PRAISE FOR *ALL IN*

'A clarion call to shed the masks we wear and embrace our true selves. This book is a powerful guide to finding love – authentic, transformative love – by first learning to love who we are. It is a must-read for anyone who is ready to embrace vulnerability and step into a life full of love, joy and soulful connection.'

MANDY McELHINNEY, actor

'This book is such a generous offering to the world and to the gay community so in need of hearing these wise words. By calling out all the hurdles that still exist for gay men trying to navigate a heteronormative environment, we breathe out a collective sigh of relief.'

NADINE GARNER, actor

'A heartfelt journey that intertwines Vinko's personal story with insightful advice on how to truly connect and find love. My eyes were opened to the differences between heterosexual relationships and those experienced by gay men. It gave voice to struggles I hadn't fully understood before, and in doing so, moved me. For anyone outside the gay community, this book is a clear window into the emotional landscape, challenges, and beauty of love in a world that still too often misunderstand.'

JACQUI BACKER, marketing strategist

'A powerful celebration of love and connection on your own terms. Vinko offers heartfelt wisdom and practical tips that resonate across all relationships – inviting us to love, listen, and trust more deeply.'

KATIE COLLINS, entertainment agent

'A gem of guidance and enlightenment in a world of doubt and judgement, for LGBTQ+ community and beyond.'

KAREN DOUGHMAN, business woman

'This book is for anyone who wants to build deeper connections and to live this one precious life, fully. Vinko gives us tools to live by. After reading this book I started using them in all my relationships and instantly experienced the benefits.'

HAYLEY McELHINNEY, actor

VINKO ANTHONY was born in Croatia (then Yugoslavia), in 1971 and immigrated to Australia in 1983. From an early age, he showed a strong entrepreneurial spirit – already running small businesses at the age of thirteen while still studying. This drive eventually evolved into founding his own global company at the age of 40. Over the years, he has built a truly international career, wearing many hats across different fields – from high-end fashion to alternative medicine, healing and yoga. What has always defined Vinko's world are the friendships he has nurtured and his deep belief in making life a more joyful, meaningful place for others. Alongside his business ventures and life experiences, Vinko has always been writing and painting.

This book brings together his personal journey, professional path and relationships, with the intention of inspiring others to live fully and embrace life with love and authenticity.

Vinko lives in Sydney with his husband, Andrea.

VINKO ANTHONY

How to make love stick

BEAU BRUMMELL
PROFESSIONAL / INTRODUCTIONS

First published in Australia in 2025 by Vinko Anthony
info@beaubrummellintroductions.com

Copyright © Vinko Anthony, 2025
The moral rights of the author have been asserted.

A catalogue record for this work is available from the National Library of Australia

ISBN: 978-1-7638250-6-2 (Paperback)
ISBN: 978-1-7638250-7-9 (Ebook)

All rights reserved. Except as permitted under the *Australian Copyright Act 1968* (for example, fair dealing for the purposes of study, research, criticism or review) no part of this book may be reproduced, stored in a retrieval system, communicated or transmitted in any form or by any means without prior written permission from the author. All enquiries should be made to the author: info@beaubrummellintroductions.com

Produced by Bernadette Foley, Broadcast Books, www.broadcastbooks.com.au
Proofread by Puddingburn Publishing Services
Cover and text design by Melanie Feddersen, i2i Design, i2i.com.au
Typeset in Times New Roman 10.5/17pt by i2i Design
Cover and author photograph, page iii, by Sealy Brandt
Printed by IngramSpark

Beau Brummell Introductions, Suite 402/24–30 Springfield Avenue,
Potts Point, NSW, Australia, 2011

beaubrummellintroductions.com

The names and identifying characteristics of some people in this book have been changed.

Broadcast Books acknowledges Aboriginal and Torres Strait Islander peoples as the first storytellers of this nation and the Traditional Custodians of the land on which we live and work. We acknowledge their continuing culture and pay our respects to Elders past and present.

CONTENTS

Introduction ix
CHAPTER ONE All-in love **1**
CHAPTER TWO Listening skills **39**
CHAPTER THREE Carnivals and masks **69**
CHAPTER FOUR Love and connection **85**
CHAPTER FIVE Self-hatred **103**
CHAPTER SIX Dating with HIV **123**
CHAPTER SEVEN Jouissance: Pleasure beyond safety **145**
CHAPTER EIGHT Figuring it all out **161**
CHAPTER NINE Relationships and marriage **175**
The all-in ending **189**
Beau Brummell Introductions **194**
Acknowledgments **196**

INTRODUCTION

When my partner Andrea walked into my life, everything changed. For the very first time, I was 'all in'. I knew I would do whatever it took to create a life full of love with Andrea. And it took a lot.

Andrea inspired this book, just as he restored my passion for understanding the true power of love, listening and emotional growth. From our first days together, Andrea's presence has challenged me to look deeper into my assumptions about how I live and what I think, to listen more intently, and to embrace the belief that, with love and understanding, anything is possible.

And we have put that promise to the test. We have built two global businesses and created communities and homes in three countries: Croatia (my birthplace), Italy (his) and Australia, our chosen home.

Andrea is a big reason I am who I am today, and his influence is woven into every page you're about to read. It's all too easy to forget to acknowledge to ourselves and to our lover how much they mean to us, and that is why I wrote those words. Thank you, Andrea, for being the man who could do that for me.

I wanted to write a book about the power of that kind of affirmation. *All In* is the story of how I learned to love and how Andrea and I now suggest that our clients learn to love each other. Because one of the businesses that Andrea and I started is Beau Brummell Introductions, a dating and matchmaking service.

For gay men, the journey to 'All-in' love is often complicated by unique challenges. We navigate a social context where homophobia, both overt and subtle, can seep into our internal narratives, fostering self-hatred, shame and depression.

This book confronts these internal struggles head-on, recognising that the way the world treats us often shapes how we see ourselves.

I explore how self-hatred manifests – through negative self-talk, avoidant behaviours and destructive actions – and how dating apps, with their emphasis on appearance and superficial traits, can intensify these feelings of inadequacy. Healing from self-hatred requires self-compassion, challenging our inner critic, building confidence, and finding supportive communities that affirm our worth.

My own journey has been marked by such challenges, particularly around disclosing my HIV status. This deeply personal experience, which I share openly in these pages, highlights the fear and stigma that many gay men face. It underscores the importance of education, empathy, and creating safe spaces where individuals can find love and acceptance without judgement. The concept of 'U=U' (undetectable = untransmittable) is a medical breakthrough that has transformed lives, yet the emotional burden of disclosure remains. This book advocates for a world where HIV status does not hinder the search for love, emphasising that true connections transcend health conditions.

I also delve into the symbolic role of 'carnival and masks' in gay culture. Carnivals offer a liberating space for self-expression and identity exploration, where masks can be both protection and a means of revealing deeper truths. However, the chapter 'Carnivals and masks' cautions against masks becoming a permanent habit, obscuring our true selves and hindering genuine connections.

Ultimately, this book is a call to courage – the courage to unmask, to confront self-hatred, to embrace vulnerability, and to truly listen to ourselves and others. It's about building a life where love is not just a feeling but a conscious choice, a powerful force that enables us to live fully, deeply and authentically, inspiring others to do the same.

WE ARE ALL MORE THAN THE MAN WE DATE

This book is about dating and relationships. And it is about more than that.

It is about the way you approach life itself. It is about the social context we face as gay men and the impact that context has on our love lives and partners. It is about the special challenges we face, such as HIV, and about our culture and its wonderful attributes, such as the carnivals we foster and the masks we don.

When I met Andrea Zaza, I realised that the solution to love's woes wasn't about finding the right person but about becoming the right person. I had to become the man that attracted the love I wanted. The key wasn't to make more of an effort, but to try a different approach. How? It starts with listening. It's all about listening. It is about listening to your man and listening to yourself. Make listening about connection and you will find love.

This book, and the journey behind our businesses, was born from the moment we found each other.

We had both spent years in relationships that, deep down, weren't right. And sometimes, you can feel more alone in the wrong relationship than you do on your own. Swiping left and right was never going to lead to an equal, real partnership. We both knew that if we ever left the relationships we were in at that time, it had to be for something real, something better, and without fully realising it at the time, our commitment to each other also planted the seed for what would later become our business.

This book is born out of that realisation. Perhaps like you, we once had people around us, but we still felt something was missing. We didn't want a life of endless swiping, making instant judgements, chasing instead of connecting. What changed is that we became ready to stop surviving and start thriving, ready to stop chasing and start attracting the love, the life, and the future we truly wanted. And that's what we want for you too.

I want to help you simplify desire to what I truly believe it is: a search for connection. A search for someone who sees you for all that you are (the strong and the weak parts) and loves you anyway. In my experience, the deeper the connection, the hotter the sex.

The noise around us gets louder as the tech gets faster. We are bombarded with information, opinions and expectations. I want to bring you back to the simplicity of love. The most important aspect of connection. To listen, to ourselves, to others, and to the subtle messages that life sends our way. Ears are for more than nibbling. They open the door to the sexiest connections you ever had.

As you read this book, give yourself the gift of time. Time to reflect, to understand, and to change the way you approach every interaction. Save your energy by focusing on what matters and making decisions that bring you closer to your goals. You can become the hero of your own love story.

In the many years of running BBI, Andrea and I have helped our clients navigate the complexities of love and relationships. I've seen the struggles and the heartbreaks, and the triumphs and the moments of profound connection.

My own journey to fulfilling love hasn't been without its challenges. Coming out as gay, finding my way in a world that didn't always understand me, and then realising that the power to change my life was within me are all experiences that shaped who I am and fuel my passion for helping others.

I'm so excited for you to dive in. Each chapter will take you a step closer to a life filled with love. As you turn these pages, you'll discover tools and strategies that help change the limiting beliefs that have held you back. These aren't abstract concepts; they're actionable steps you can take to transform your life.

For example, I dedicate an entire chapter to the art of listening. Listening is about more than hearing the words; it's about truly engaging with another person's experience. It's about creating a space where both of you can be honest and in which understanding flourishes. This ability to listen transforms your relationships. You will shift from reacting to what life brings your way to creating the life you want.

The journey you're about to embark on is one of self-discovery, of understanding others, and of building a life filled with love, joy and endless possibilities.

With love and understanding as your guiding principles, you'll find that some hopes you thought were impossible become possible. Personal challenges, deeper connections, or the courage to pursue your dreams. Everything becomes attainable when you believe in the affirming power of love.

Writing this book has been character building for me, to say the least. English is my second language. But I love to write, and it's been a wonderful experience for me to pull together my jottings, my thoughts and my life experiences.

In these pages, you'll find my story, and the stories of the incredible people who have inspired me, the friends who have walked alongside me, and the moments that have shaped my belief in the power of love and freedom.

Whether you're at the beginning of your journey or seeking to deepen the connections you already have, I hope this book inspires, uplifts, and guides you towards the life your heart has always known was possible.

TO HOPE OR NOT TO HOPE

Imagine, if you will, sitting across from a new date. Excited? Yes. Hopeful? Absolutely. Struggling with nagging doubt. Sadly, yes. Will this conversation lead anywhere meaningful? Does he really get me, or is this just another shallow exchange?

Perhaps you have noticed that you struggle to make your relationships work, or to find the kind of love you want. Even when you decide to seek deeper connections and search for more meaning in your life, it's not easy to overcome your fears.

Now try an experiment. Think back to a time when you felt truly heard, when someone listened to the words you said, understood them and understood the emotions and thoughts behind them. How powerful was that connection? Moments like that shape your life and relationships. I want to show you that these moments need not be rare; they can be the foundation of every relationship you build.

The answers are within your reach. As you journey through this book, I want you to feel the inspiration that Andrea brought into my life and I bought into his. I hope in doing so, you will see how you can transform the way you connect with yourself and with friends and lovers in your life. You will discover how to 'listen' with your heart, think with clarity, and create the life and the relationship you've always dreamed of. This is your moment. Start now.

CHAPTER ONE

All-in love

Love is about being 'all in'.

'All in' means commitment. Andrea and I believe in the power of commitment to foster the deepest kind of intimacy between loving partners. When you open yourself to committed romantic love, it is a heavenly place to be. You feel a profound union, a mutual appreciation and an acceptance of each other's true selves. This reciprocal admiration and acceptance make everything fall into place, creating a harmonious and deeply fulfilling romantic relationship. We believe so strongly that the strongest connections are fostered when two individuals commit and then communicate with each other in their authentic voices.

Our legacy is etched in the lives we touch in our work every day, the love we ignite, and the belief that each person possesses a capacity for deep connection. Andrea and I are not into love defined by others. Finding a life partner doesn't mean moulding oneself to the desires of another but about discovering a shared song.

This book is not so much a guide to dating, but a guide to understanding love, what helps you to find love, and what helps you to stick at it. And, in the end, that is our philosophy of dating. Come along with us and you, too, can find someone to sing with.

All In also looks at the social context of love that we, as gay men, find ourselves in. A big part of what we do at our agency, Beau Brummell Introductions, is to educate our clients about the social pressures that work for and against them, and how our mental and physical health, including HIV, can have a deep impact on our approach to love and relationships. These issues cannot be ignored.

In this opening chapter, I will give you a bird's eye view of the topics that I explore throughout the book. It is not a textbook. I am writing to light a fire in you, a fire of desire for love, sex and intimacy with the man in your life, or the man who soon will be in your life. To get to that desire, I look at love with friends, love (and toxicity) with family, love for yourself, and even a list of what I believe are the 'essentials' for a successful romantic partnership. These lessons in love are our gifts from the 1500 couples who have found happiness through working with us and from the work that Andrea and I have done together so far.

Romantic love differs from other expressions of love in a single important way. When you elevate one relationship to that of a life partnership with a sexual dimension, you are in a romantic relationship, at least as far as we are concerned.

But to love your partner well, you must understand yourself in all expressions of love. Love manifests in many other forms and the common three are friendships, familial bonds and self-love. Each expression of love contributes to your overall understanding of love, and all expressions are crucial if you want to fully comprehend and nurture your romantic partnership.

The way you experience and express love in different relationships – whether it be with friends, family or through self-love – shapes your capacity to connect deeply and authentically with a romantic partner. From your friends, family and self you learn the empathy and patience that bring a deeper connection to your partner. You navigate challenges with grace, celebrate joys with sincerity, and build a lasting bond based on genuine affection and respect.

MEET ANDREA, LOVE OF MY LIFE

From the moment Andrea and I met, our love was immediate and powerful. Andrea understood my dreams and shared them. I found in him a soulmate whose kindness and creativity mirrored my aspirations. It was as if we had known each other our entire lives.

We had been together for ten years at the time I started to write this book and had achieved what many could only dream of (if I say so myself). We have opened two international businesses, one being our dating agency. The other is our architecture company Zaza Architecture, based in Croatia. Andrea trained as an architect in Rome, Italy, and worked in Vienna, Austria, for a long time. I have a varied background, as you will learn, and have built solid business acumen from its variety.

Our success has not been without challenges. Navigating the ever-changing global economic landscape built our resilience and adaptability. We faced numerous obstacles, from financial crises to intense competition. Yet our dedication to each other and our unwavering belief in our shared vision kept us moving forward.

We have bought three properties that symbolise our journey together. Our home is in the heart of Sydney, where we live and love, which is right across the road from our office. Our office, a sleek and modern building, testifies to our professional achievements and is a hub of creativity and innovation. And our holiday home, a charming house on an island on the Croatian coast, is a beautiful villa, overlooking the Adriatic Sea. Here is a sanctuary where we can escape the world and find solace in each other's company.

As lovely as these achievements sounds, and as important as they are to us, it is our dedication to our families, friends and clients that provides us with the strength to overcome every obstacle. Our backgrounds as migrants to Australia and the challenges we faced coming out as gay men instilled in us a profound resilience. Together, we have created a circle of positivity and support that extends beyond our personal relationship.

Our businesses thrive because we commit to excellence and genuinely care for our clients. We treat every project, no matter how big or small, with the same level of passion and dedication. This approach has earned us a loyal client base and a reputation for reliability and innovation.

The love between Andrea and me is the foundation upon which we have built our lives and careers. Our love story is about both romantic gestures and shared dreams and about facing the harsh realities of life together. We believe that love is not just a feeling but a choice, a decision to stand by each other through thick and thin.

Our days are filled with the hustle and bustle of running businesses and managing properties, but we always make time for each other. Whether it is a quiet dinner at home, a stroll through the vineyards of Croatia, or a late-night brainstorming session at our office, we cherish every moment together.

Our friends and Andrea's family are an integral part of our romantic journey. Andrea and I both love socialising with our friends. The gatherings we host bring people together in celebration of love and life. We believe in the importance of community and the power of collective support.

In the end, our love conquered every challenge that life threw our way. It gave us the courage to dream big, the resilience to face adversity and the joy of living a life full of possibilities. We are proud to offer our journey as an example of how love, when nurtured and cherished, can truly make anything possible.

THE BLACK T-SHIRTS OF LOVE

In every man's wardrobe is a black t-shirt or two. This item of clothing is the basic, the essential. You just can't do life without your basic black t-shirt. I want to introduce you to the three black t-shirts of love: trust, independence and conflict. Yes, that's right. Conflict is a basic and if you don't get it right, you can't do love.

Trust is the foundation

Romantic relationships are all about trust. Trust is the foundation upon which all healthy relationships are built. But what is trust? Trust is the feeling of being secure and valued. It's the outcome of your behaviours. You build trust when you are reliable, open and honest with your partner, friends, family and yourself. When your trust in each other is strong, you will find it so much easier to navigate the inevitable challenges that arise in long-term partnerships. Yes, they happen to the best of us.

But why is trust so important to an all-in relationship? Because with trust comes intimacy. I do not just mean physical intimacy and sex, although that is a huge part of it. Intimacy in romantic relationships encompasses emotional, intellectual and even spiritual connections. When you trust your partner with your thoughts, dreams and fears, you foster a deep bond and understanding. With time, communication and affection, intimacy flourishes. And I can't stress the affection part enough. Your attentive presence shows your partner they are cherished and significant in your life.

All long-term partnerships require resilience and adaptability. We are all, in our own ways, challenging to live with. And life is unpredictable. Relationships are bound to encounter obstacles, both internal and external. With a solid foundation of trust and intimacy, you and your partner will face these challenges as a united front. I will talk a lot about communication in this book. That is what reinforces trust and intimacy, a safe space where both partners feel heard and respected. Trust isn't something that arrives all at once; it's something you build, brick by brick, through the small choices you make every day. I've learned this both in my own life and in watching countless couples find their rhythm together.

The first thing is consistency. It sounds simple, but it's powerful. When you say you'll call, call. When you make plans, show up. Every time you follow through, you're telling your partner without words: *You can rely on me.* Over time, those little actions stack up into something solid and safe.

Another part is honesty, even when it's uncomfortable. It's easy to share the good news, the parts of ourselves we're proud of. But the real intimacy comes when you can sit down and say, 'This is where I'm struggling', or 'This is what scares me.' It's in those vulnerable moments that trust deepens – because your partner sees that you're not putting on a mask, you're letting him in.

Listening matters just as much. Not listening to reply but listening to really hear. When your partner feels that their thoughts, feelings and worries land in a safe place with you, they begin to trust that they don't need to hold back.

And finally, patience. Trust isn't built overnight, and sometimes it grows unevenly – one of you might be ready to open up more quickly than the other. That's okay. What matters is holding the space, staying steady, and letting trust unfold at its own pace.

If I had to put it simply: trust is built in the small things, it deepens in the vulnerable things, and it lasts when you handle it with care.

When Andrea and I first began building our life together, there were moments when trust wasn't built on grand gestures, but on the quiet, everyday choices. I still recall the times when I shared fears I'd never spoken aloud before – fears about family, about being accepted, about being truly seen. Instead of brushing them aside, Andrea listened. He didn't try to fix everything, he just made me feel safe enough to let it out. Those moments changed something between us. They taught me that trust isn't about pretending to be strong all the time – it's about daring to be soft and discovering that the other person will meet you there, gently.

That's why I tell people: don't underestimate the power of those small, ordinary acts. It's often in the little things that love proves itself trustworthy.

Independence becomes interdependence

Maintaining a balance between independence and togetherness is essential. It's called interdependence. You have the freedom to pursue your personal interests and growth, as well as the goals and activities that you share. You will know you have this balance right when you feel a clear individual identity within the relationship, and don't fall prey to feelings of suffocation. When both partners are committed to these principles, they create a resilient and fulfilling partnership that stands the test of time.

Conflict in romantic relationships

Disputes in romantic love and partner relationships are inevitable. They arise from different perspectives, needs and desires. They are also a natural part of any intimate relationship and contribute to your growth as a person. Conflict strengthens your romantic bond if handled constructively.

Some common conflict triggers include communication breakdowns, unmet expectations, financial disagreements, differences in values or beliefs, and external stressors such as work or family issues. Whenever these differences surface, you will find misunderstandings, frustration and emotional distress.

What's the answer? Effective communication. Easy, right? Wrong. While open, honest and respectful dialogue allows both partners to express their feelings and perspectives without fear of judgement or retaliation, it's hard to do.

That said, if I had to boil down successful love to a single ingredient, I would say it is your ability to listen. When you learn to listen 'actively' (a technique we explore later in the book) and with empathy, you will quickly break through conflict to understand each other's viewpoints and find common ground.

Conflict is constructive when both parties stay calm, avoid blame, focus on the issue rather than on past grievances and seek solutions that satisfy both partners. (Easier said than done.) Compromise and collaborate and you will reach a mutually acceptable resolution.

Not all disputes can be resolved immediately. Some take ongoing negotiation and adjustment. Patience and persistence are important, as is the willingness to revisit discussions as often as you need to.

When you navigate conflict with your partner, you demonstrate your commitment to him, yourself, and the relationship, and you both deepen your emotional connection and enhance your understanding of each other.

That said, you might get stuck. Some disputes reveal deep unresolved issues best unravelled with professional help. Couple's therapy or counselling will give you both new tools and strategies for managing conflicts and improving communication. Seeking help is not a sign of failure, but of maturity and commitment.

THE OTHER 10 MUST-HAVES FOR A THRIVING ROMANTIC RELATIONSHIP

Okay, I have outlined the big three essentials, the black t-shirts of love: trust, interdependence and conflict skills. However, in our experience, there are a bunch of other must-haves, 10 in all, that make your relationship stick. So, I want to provide you with a quick reference guide in the list below for when times are tough. If you and your partner hit a rough patch, focus on restoring the top three first. Then reread these additional essentials and start working on them.

1. **Communication:** Share your thoughts, feelings and experiences with your partner. Listen actively (see Chapter 2) to their perspectives without judgement.
2. **Quality time:** Spend time doing activities you both enjoy and create new shared experiences. Whether it's a date night, a weekend getaway or simple daily routines, being present with each other fosters intimacy and connection.

3. **Mutual respect:** Respect each other's individuality, opinions and boundaries. Acknowledge and appreciate your partner's strengths and contributions to the relationship.
4. **Emotional support:** Be there for your partner during both good times and challenging moments. Offer encouragement, empathy and comfort. Emotional support helps both partners feel valued and understood.
5. **Shared goals and values:** Discuss and align your long-term goals and values. Having a shared vision for the future provides direction and purpose in your relationship. These might be big or small: buying a house, or going on a cycling holiday.
6. **Intimacy:** Foster both physical and emotional intimacy. Physical intimacy includes affection, touch and sexual connection, while emotional intimacy involves sharing your deepest thoughts, fears and dreams.
7. **Express love and appreciation:** Regularly express your love and appreciation for your partner. Small gestures, words of affirmation and acts of kindness go a long way towards making your partner feel cherished and valued.
8. **Share responsibilities:** Equitably share responsibilities and tasks, whether they are household chores, financial obligations or caregiving duties. This builds a sense of teamwork and mutual respect.
9. **Humour and fun:** Don't forget to have fun together. Laughter and playful moments strengthen your bond and make the relationship more enjoyable.

10. **Continuous learning:** Be open to learning and growing together. Attend workshops, read books or seek advice on relationship-building. Show your commitment to improving and deepening your connection.

LEARN LOVE THROUGH FRIENDS, FAMILY AND YOURSELF

Friendships teach you about trust, loyalty and support. Familial bonds often show you unconditional love, sacrifice and enduring connections. Self-love, perhaps the most foundational love, is about recognising your own worth, setting boundaries and nurturing your personal growth, something I will cover in much more detail later in this book. Each form of love contributes to a comprehensive understanding of what it means to love and be loved.

In our experience, the quality of your friendships, family relationships and your relationship with yourself make a big difference in your ability to be 'all in' in your romantic relationship. These other expressions of love determine how you engage in a romantic partnership. You might struggle with vulnerability, communication or maintaining a healthy balance between independence and intimacy. For instance, without self-love, you might depend on your partner for validation, which will put a lot of pressure on the relationship. Alternatively, without understanding the nuances of friendship, you might overlook the importance of companionship and mutual respect in your romantic relationship.

In understanding and embracing different expressions of love, you become more aware of your needs, strengths and areas for growth. You then can bring your whole, authentic self into the romantic relationship, fostering a deeper and more meaningful connection. You learn to give and receive love in a way that is enriching and sustainable, ensuring that your relationship is built on a foundation of mutual understanding and genuine affection.

The chosen bonds that sustain us
If love is the home we build, then friendships are the beams that keep the roof standing tall.

Throughout my life, friendships have been my greatest gift, my chosen family, my sanctuary. Long before Andrea came into my life, it was my friends who nurtured my spirit, challenged my ideas, listened without judgement, and laughed alongside me even in the most uncertain times. And once Andrea and I found each other, our friendships – mine, his and ours together – became the vital threads that strengthen the fabric of our relationship.

Friendships have been, and always will be, the life force behind everything meaningful I create.

The Italian circle: Teaching each other through others
One of the most beautiful chapters of my relationship with Andrea unfolded through his circle of Italian friends. Spending time with them taught me so much about Andrea's humour, his stubbornness, his passions, the layers that no one person can

reveal on their own. They showed me his history, his nuances, the spirit he carried long before he met me.

There is a magic in seeing the person you love through the eyes of those who have loved them across time and space. His friends helped me understand him better, and in many ways, they made me love him even more.

Shared laughter over long dinners, chaotic group gatherings and travels, heated debates, and affectionate teasing became a mirror through which I could see not only Andrea but myself, too. The generosity and openness of that Italian group reminded me of how crucial it is to nurture friendships, not just individually but together as a couple. It also reminded me so much of my years as a child growing up in Croatia. I think this is a big reason why Andrea and I understand each other. I've seen time and time again, not only in my own life but in the lives of many of the clients we've worked with, that you can tell so much about a person by the way they are with their friends. Meeting your partner's circle isn't just a social formality – it's a window into who they really are. When you sit with them in that space, when you see them laugh at old jokes or slip into the comfort of long-standing friendships, you're witnessing the unpolished, unfiltered version of them. You see how they give and receive, how they listen, and how they show up for the people who matter most.

And then there's the other side of it – bringing your partner into *your* circle can make you feel vulnerable. It's almost like saying, 'Here I am, in full colour, surrounded by the people who've seen me at my best and at my worst. This is the rest of my story.' But it's also one of the most powerful steps you can take in weaving someone into your life. Friends are, in many ways, the chosen family who hold your history. When you invite your partner into that space, you're not just sharing your past, you're starting to create a shared present.

Some of the strongest relationships I've seen didn't just grow in the quiet of two people getting to know each other – they blossomed when those two worlds of friends began to mix. A casual dinner, a Sunday afternoon catch-up, a trip away with a group … those are the moments when bonds deepen in ways no fancy date night ever could.

So, if you're wondering how to strengthen your connection, don't underestimate the power of community. Love is built between two people, yes, but it's nourished, supported and celebrated by the circles that surround you.

The unbreakable bond that shaped my life
When I think about the friendships that have truly shaped my life, one person stands above all: David. To even call him a friend feels too small; David is part of who I am. He is the one who saw and understood my kindness at a time when many misunderstood or took it for granted. In doing so, he extended to me a friendship so pure and boundless that it has become one of the defining relationships of my life.

We are, in many ways, very different people. Yet the admiration and respect between us are total, unwavering and unconditional. David has trusted me in ways that very few ever have. He has supported me through every challenge, often more than any family member ever thought to, and certainly more than I could have ever asked for. Everything I have built, every step forward I have taken, carries traces of his belief in me. Without him, I would not be who I am today.

Friends like David do not often come along in life. Love, loyalty and trust like this are rare, almost mythical. He has taught me some of my greatest life lessons, especially about strength. In relationships, in life, he showed me how to be tougher, how to stand firmer when needed. At the same time, I know he often leans on my softer side, for advice, for perspective, just as I lean on his strength when I need to be reminded of my own power. We are two very different spirits, but together, we balance one another in a way only true chosen family can.

David is proof that family isn't always the one you are born into, sometimes, it's the souls you find along the way who recognise you, believe in you, and love you into becoming who you were always meant to be. And for me, he has been that and so much more.

The sanctuary of chosen family
Growing up, I learned early that family wasn't always determined by blood. While I hold gratitude for where I came from, it was my friends who, over the years, filled the spaces where understanding, acceptance and unconditional love were missing. They celebrated the milestones with me, mourned the losses, sat with me through silent storms, and challenged me

to be better when I needed it most. They became my family, a family of choice, not circumstance.

This idea of 'chosen family' is something that Andrea and I both instinctively understood. From the very beginning, our lives were filled with extraordinary people who weren't just guests in our story, they were co-authors. We treat our friendships with the same reverence and devotion we treat each other, knowing that love, in all its forms, deserves care, presence, and celebration.

Among all the beautiful connections Andrea and I share, none has been quite as profound as our bond with Baci, Monte and Peter. They are not just friends; they are family in a way that words often fall short of capturing. We just about live together, we travel together, and we co-parent Monte as though he were our own puppy. I truly could not imagine life without them.

They have been present in every entanglement of our relationship, every joy, every tear, every high, and every low. Through them, we've experienced what it means to be fully supported, fully understood, and fully loved by those who choose you, not out of obligation but out of genuine, unwavering affection. They have shown Andrea and me that real family transcends titles and expectations; it's built in the daily acts of care, trust, and unbreakable presence.

Some of us are lucky to have profound people in our lives, and for over 30 years, Eileen has been a guiding light in mine. Her wisdom, presence and unwavering support through yoga have shaped not just my practice, but the person I've become.

A perfect moment of imperfection

Of course, no relationship is without its imperfections, including my own tendency to slip into perfectionism.

One afternoon, in the midst of one of my 'Andrea should be doing more' monologues, my dear friend Narelle, one of the wisest, kindest funniest souls to ever walk into my life, looked at me with a smile and said, 'Vinko, but ... would you let him?'

We both burst out laughing, because she was right. Sometimes, the problem wasn't that Andrea wasn't doing enough; it was that I had such a firm grip on how everything 'should' be done, that even when he wanted to help, there wasn't any space left for him.

Narelle has always had this gift of cutting through my noise with humour and grace. Her words that day have stayed with me. Every time I catch myself edging towards control, I remember her voice, her smile, and that gentle truth.

Nadine, my north star

Then there's Nadine. There aren't enough pages in the world to capture what her friendship has meant to me.

She has been my lighthouse in every storm, a silent strength that anchored me even when my world felt chaotic. Nadine has helped me navigate not just my relationship with Andrea, but every major crossroad in my life. Her ability to love without expectation, to give without keeping score, has always been a lesson in grace.

She reminds me that true friendship, like true love, is about presence, not performance. It's about showing up, not about measuring outcomes.

When I needed to reflect on past relationships, she offered a space of honesty and non-judgement. When I doubted my path, she believed for me until I could believe again for myself.

Nadine is one of those rare friends who doesn't demand that you shrink or perform, she just asks you to be.

The theatre of life: Strong women and gentle souls
It's not an accident that so many of my closest friends have been thespians, artists, creatives. There's something about the vulnerability of artists that speaks to me. They are used to living with their hearts outside their bodies, just like I do.

Strong women have always surrounded me. Women who dared to live boldly, who carried their scars like medals, who knew how to cry and laugh in the same breath. They grounded me when I became too rigid. They challenged me when I thought I had it all figured out. They offered wisdom born of resilience, creativity, and fire.

My personality has always suited people who are a little raw, a little tender. Vulnerability doesn't scare me; it draws me closer. And in those friendships, I found mirrors, mentors, and muses. Katie Collins was the first real friend I made in Australia, and through her, my entire life here truly began. She opened my world to so much: to the arts, to dance, to the energy of the nightlife, to a side of Australia I might never have found on my own. Through Katie, I didn't just find places or experiences; I found a sense of belonging. Our bond has become something that time and distance can never break. We share history, memories, and a love that is woven into every chapter of my story here. Without her, my journey in Australia would have been a very different one, and for everything she brought into my life, I am forever grateful.

FRIENDSHIP AND RELATIONSHIPS: KEEPING SEPARATE LIVES ALIVE

One of the most important lessons I've learned, and something Andrea and I both hold sacred, is the importance of maintaining separate lives, even within the intimacy of a shared life.

We believe deeply in the idea that two whole people create the healthiest partnership. Not two halves completing each other, but two entire beings walking side by side.

Friendships are essential in preserving that wholeness. They offer perspectives outside the echo chamber of the relationship. They keep you curious, growing, connected to the broader world. They remind you that you are more than someone's partner; you are also a friend, a dreamer, a seeker, an individual.

Sharing friends together, travelling, celebrating, grieving, adds another layer of connection. For Andrea and me, some of our best memories are of times spent with our friends: wine-fuelled evenings under foreign skies, long road trips filled with bad playlists and good conversations, helping each other pack up lives and move into new homes, laughing until our sides hurt over some private, ridiculous joke.

Those shared experiences have created a kind of extended family for us, a village that we cherish and protect.

WHEN FRIENDSHIPS END: LOSS AND LIBERATION

Of course, not all friendships are forever.

There is a particular kind of heartbreak that comes from losing a friend, sometimes sharper, sometimes more confusing, than the end of a romantic relationship.

I've learned that friendships, like all living things, have their seasons. Some grow with you, stretch into new versions of themselves. Some wither when they no longer have the soil they need to thrive.

Letting go of a friendship can be one of the hardest things to do. The guilt, the sadness, the 'what ifs'. But it's also profoundly liberating when you recognise that some connections, once so vital, are now chains that keep you from moving forward.

When a friendship becomes a source of pain, diminishes your light, or consistently drains rather than nourishes, it's okay, necessary even, to choose your wellbeing.

Andrea and I have both experienced this. We've held each other through the mourning of friendships lost. And we've also celebrated the new space that loss creates, space for deeper authenticity, for friendships that truly uplift and inspire.

THE ONGOING TAPESTRY

Today, when I look around, I see a tapestry rich with colour, woven from decades of friendships, some new, some ancient, all cherished. I see Nadine's steady light. I hear Narelle's laughter. I feel the warmth of Andrea's Italian friends, and our shared village of beautiful souls who walk this journey with us.

Our love, Andrea's and mine, isn't isolated in a bubble. It's strengthened, nourished, and constantly renewed by the friendships we hold sacred. Every dinner table filled with friends, every late-night phone call, every spontaneous road trip or quiet afternoon on the couch, these are the bricks and beams that make our love story not just 'ours', but something bigger, something braver.

FRIENDSHIPS SUSTAIN ME. THEY SUSTAIN US

If I have learned anything, it is that to go 'all in' on love is also to go 'all in' on friendship.

Not just when it's easy. Not just when it's convenient. But always. Because love is built in community. Love flourishes where there is laughter, understanding, acceptance, forgiveness, and unwavering presence.

And there is no better way to walk this wild, beautiful life than hand-in-hand with your love, surrounded by the chosen family that makes everything sweeter, richer, and infinitely more real.

SELF-LOVE AND PERSONAL GROWTH

Self-love influences your self-esteem and mental health. Cultivating a positive relationship with yourself is crucial for building a successful romantic relationship. But what does self-love mean to you? Is it confidence, knowledge of yourself, or respect for yourself? Do you feel you need another's love to prove your self-worth? Self-love can manifest in various forms and understanding what it means to you is the first step towards nurturing it.

Self-esteem

Self-esteem is intertwined with self-love. It encompasses confidence in yourself, a belief in your abilities, and a thorough knowledge of your values and boundaries. You understand what to settle for and what not to settle for. Self-esteem is shaped by your intrinsic belief about yourself, how you view the world, and how you interact with it. It impacts your decisions, relationships and overall life satisfaction.

I didn't wake up one day with self-esteem neatly packed and ready to go. For me, it's been a slow, sometimes clumsy, sometimes beautiful journey. And if I'm honest, I think most people are still learning how to hold it firmly, even when life tries to shake it out of their hands.

One of the first things that helped me was learning to keep small promises to myself. Nothing dramatic. Just the little things: if I said I'd go for a walk in the morning, I went. If I told myself I'd call a friend back, I did. Each time I followed through, it was like laying down a small brick in the foundation of how I saw myself. Slowly, those bricks started to feel like something solid I could stand on.

Another turning point was changing the way I spoke to myself. For years, my inner voice was harsher than I'd ever dream of being to anyone else. I wouldn't have let a friend speak to me the way I was speaking to myself daily. So I began to catch it, to gently swap those words for kinder ones. At first it felt awkward, almost fake. But over time, I realised kindness to myself wasn't a luxury – it was the fuel that made me braver in the world.

And maybe the most powerful thing was surrounding myself with people who truly saw me. The kind of friends who remind you of your worth even when you can't see it. We often think self-esteem is something we build all on our own, but the truth is, we borrow it sometimes. We borrow it from the people who love us, until we're strong enough to carry it ourselves.

Self-esteem, to me, isn't about arrogance or pretending you've got it all figured out. It's about holding yourself gently, keeping your word to yourself, and remembering you are worthy of kindness – especially your own.

Mental health
While a sensitive topic, mental health is integral to this discussion. In this context, mental health refers to your personal happiness, "a sense of security and feeling safe in your own skin. This isn't about episodes of mental illness that require professional treatment but about your day-to-day emotional wellbeing. Cultivating self-love will enhance your mental health as you foster a positive inner dialogue, reduce stress and increase resilience.

When you are positive and excited about yourself and who you are, you not only manifest positivity in others but also nurture your own wellbeing. This optimistic outlook creates a ripple effect, influencing those around you and enhancing your interactions with them. Your enthusiasm and self-assurance can inspire and uplift others, fostering a supportive and encouraging environment.

Working to improve yourself as a person is about more than just self-improvement – it's about growth, resilience and a deeper understanding of your values and potential. For example, I started working on my mental health with regular exercise, reading and surrounding myself with people who inspire me. I have found that when I have invested time and effort into becoming a version of myself that I feel proud of, I developed skills and qualities that helped me navigate life's challenges. I became more adaptable, patient and compassionate, not only with others but with myself as well.

Each step you take towards self-improvement builds your self-esteem and mental health, reinforcing the belief that you are capable and worthy of success and happiness. Reflecting on your achievements, practising self-compassion and surrounding yourself with supportive people are also powerful strategies. By actively working on these aspects, you create a nurturing environment for yourself, promoting both your self-esteem and mental health.

Self-love is an ongoing journey. It requires patience and practice, but the rewards – a happier, healthier and more secure you – are worth the effort. A positive self-view empowers you to face life's challenges with grace. Instead of being overwhelmed by obstacles, you start to see them as opportunities. This shift in perspective means you tackle problems more creatively and persistently, leading to better outcomes.

Space for yourself

For the past 30 years, I have practised two hours of yoga and meditation almost every day; like every practice you fall in and out of it, but it always finds you coming back. This practice helps me make difficult decisions and sustain life and love, because it allows me to feel more centred and less reactive. It provides me with the space, time and freedom to navigate life's challenges.

Dedicating two hours a day to such practices might seem unachievable. But what if I told you that incorporating even a small amount of yoga and meditation into your daily routine could give you time back and offer you the best chance to cultivate a wonderful relationship? It's the commitment to yourself, your inner world and your health and stability that such a practice represents that makes the difference.

Think of all the time you dedicate every day to feeling inadequate and out of sorts. If you would like to try turning over some of that time to the various practices available, you'll be astonished at the results. Yoga and meditation practices range from active styles to more still and introspective ones. Speak with practitioners, read about the different approaches, and find the one that resonates most with your personality and lifestyle.

You don't have to be perfect at any practice you undertake. The key is consistency. Every time you show up for yoga or meditation, you show up for yourself. Start by dedicating just 15 minutes to your practice. Whether you attend a class, or sit quietly on your mat at home, the important thing is to make it a regular part of your day. Roll out your mat and see what happens. In these moments of stillness and mindful movement, you can connect with your inner self. Try keeping a daily measure of your overall self-esteem and sense of wellbeing, for example, giving yourself a rating out of 10. Watch whether your small commitment to a daily practice changes your self-esteem and overall wellbeing.

As you nurture your body and mind, you'll find that you become more attuned to your needs and more capable of building and maintaining healthy, fulfilling relationships.

COMING OUT

Growing up in a close-knit Croatian Catholic family, tradition was woven into every aspect of my life. Our family structure was strong and tight, centred on shared values and a deep sense of community. In our small environment, everyone knew everyone, and the church was at the heart of our social and spiritual lives. This background fostered a deep connection to heritage but brought with it a rigidity about what was acceptable.

From a young age, I felt different. As I grew older, this difference became more pronounced, bringing with it a profound sense of fear. Like many young gay men, I was haunted by the fear that coming out to my family would mean abandonment and the terrifying prospect of being alone. The worry about losing my family, my friends and the only life I had ever known haunted me.

The turning point came when I moved to London. The city's vibrant diversity and more open attitudes towards LGBTQIA+

people was a stark contrast to my conservative upbringing. This was long before modern communications; I relied on letters to communicate my thoughts and feelings. Each letter to my mamma was a carefully crafted expression that masked my inner turmoil and hinted at my growing self-acceptance.

When I felt it was time to come out, I orchestrated it through letters and a scheduled phone call. In a way, the physical distance between me and my family allowed me the emotional space to talk about my feelings with clarity and honesty. I was filled with anxiety and hope as I revealed my truth to the people I loved most.

I thought it would have been more of a shock. I wanted more drama. But my family responded with love and acceptance. My relief was immense. They assured me that our bond was unbreakable, no matter the circumstances. I had feared drama and rejection, but what I received was the compassion and understanding that my relationships with my family had been lacking in some other situations.

This newfound freedom transformed me. For the first time, I was living my life authentically, freed from hiding a fundamental part of myself. The liberation that came with living a gay life openly was a profound gift, allowing me to understand myself more clearly and fully.

The fear and struggle I endured were part of what made my coming-out story so meaningful. My family's acceptance helped me feel more self-love, but it was only possible because I had fostered a sense of self-love before I came out by living in a more supportive community. In the end, my story was not one of tragedy but of triumph. A celebration of love, acceptance and the joy of living one's truth.

Not everyone has had such a good response from their family, friends or their romantic partners. Many clients have told me, 'I try to love myself, but in all my relationships, I get to the point where everyone cheats on me, or I get ghosted. My self-esteem is deflated when these things happen. I give so much, and it isn't reciprocated.'

The dating world can be tough, especially as a gay man. This book will help you understand how to protect your self-esteem and avoid repeating the same painful patterns. You will learn to recognise early warning signs and behaviours that haven't suited you in the past and make more informed decisions about who you allow into your life. You will move on from those who don't treat you with the respect and love you deserve.

You'll discover strategies to bolster your self-esteem and maintain your sense of self-worth, even when faced with challenges in relationships. This process involves understanding your needs and not settling for less than you deserve. You'll create healthier, more fulfilling relationships that are based on mutual respect and genuine connection.

Ultimately, this journey is about empowering yourself to recognise your value by learning to love yourself, thus ensuring that your future relationships are built on a foundation of respect, trust and reciprocity. As you navigate the complexities of relationships with greater awareness and confidence, you can maintain your self-esteem and attract partners who truly appreciate and reciprocate your love.

FAMILY LOVE AND BONDS

When you examine the love shared within families, including your own parent–child relationships and your sibling bonds, you gain valuable insights into the support systems that family love provides, or does not provide. Family love is foundational, serving as our first and often most enduring model of love. At its best, it is characterised by unconditional support, deep emotional bonds and a sense of belonging that help us develop a sense of wellbeing. However, not every family dynamic is a happy one. As Leo Tolstoy wrote in *Anna Karenina*, 'All happy families are alike; each unhappy family is unhappy in its own way.'

Parental love

The love between parents and children is the most powerful and formative connection. From the earliest stages of life, parents provide support, nurturing and guidance. Ideally, this relationship is built on unconditional love. Parents should offer stability, protection and encouragement. They must teach values, instil confidence and help us navigate the complexities of life. As children, we learn to trust, communicate and form attachments based on the security and affection provided by our parents. This support system shapes our self-esteem, emotional resilience and ability to form healthy relationships in the future. Most parents fail their children from time to time. Some fail them in deep, ongoing ways.

But insecure or abusive family relationships are not a life sentence. As adults, we can change how we respond and react, often with the support of a loving partner, and with the help of professional psychologists and counsellors, if need be.

Brothers and sisters
Sibling relationships combine elements of friendship and familial loyalty. Siblings may share a deep understanding of each other's experiences, and a strong sense of camaraderie and mutual support. Siblings may be our first playmates, confidants and allies, helping us develop social skills and offering companionship throughout life. The love and support exchanged between siblings can contribute to a robust familial support system, providing a sense of continuity and belonging.

Equally, sibling relationships can foster resentment and toxic relationships. They can be our first tormentors, even if they are too young to understand the consequences of their behaviour. Despite my positive experience of coming out to my parents and siblings, I have had a tough time sustaining a caring relationship with my family, as I will explain.

TOXIC FAMILY RELATIONSHIPS

As a child, I never felt truly listened to. For as long as I can remember, I have struggled with my relationship with my mother and my siblings for different reasons. I wanted to feel support and unconditional love but instead, I often felt I was living in a battleground.

As adults, my family and I led different lives. I felt I was the one trying to keep the connections alive. Our interactions stayed on the surface, and I felt no reciprocal emotional engagement. I didn't feel fulfilled in those relationships. They became strained and unsatisfactory over time. A little of anything was always enough for my family, while I felt I could achieve more, everything was possible. My family do not easily give me, or each other, support and encouragement.

After spending time with my family, I always returned home feeling drained. The weight of those interactions followed me. The lack of mutual respect and understanding from my family made it increasingly difficult for Andrea and me to sustain a healthy and fulfilling connection with them.

My mother struggled to show respect for my relationship and often treated Andrea unkindly. This was not because we were gay; it was an issue that comes from my mother's story, which is not mine to tell. I found it incredibly challenging to handle, because both Andrea and I made every effort to be supportive and kind to her. Despite our best intentions, the situation only became more difficult, adding to the strain that was already present in my family relationships. My family's negativity had begun to bleed into my personal relationships, making me withdraw from my friendships and draining me of energy to work on our business.

I didn't decide to distance myself from my family overnight. It was a gradual realisation, a painful acknowledgment that sometimes love alone isn't enough to maintain a relationship. After a particularly heated argument with Andrea, I looked at myself in the mirror and saw the reflection of a man who was constantly on edge because my family upbringing left me always waiting for the next emotional blow.

I knew something had to change.

But the resolve to make that change came later. I remember it as if it was yesterday. It was a Friday afternoon, and I sat quietly in my office in Sydney, the soft glow of the evening sun filtering through the blinds. I had just finished yoga practice and meditation. I felt calm and still. My eyes lingered on an old photo of me and my mamma in a silver frame that had belonged to my paternal grandmother, the edges worn from years of handling. In the picture, we both wore smiles, and the love seemed palpable. Yet beneath those smiles, there had always been sadness, from when I was very young. I longed for a deeper connection and less of my mother's negativity, which had slowly seeped into my life, affecting everything I held dear. That night, I looked at the photo of me and my mother one last time before tucking it away in a drawer. I whispered a silent goodbye, not just to her but to the pain and negativity our relationship had brought into my life.

I chose love, the kind that nourishes, supports and heals. With that choice, I found a path to a happier, healthier future.

I started small, reducing contact with my family and setting firm boundaries. For example, our visits became shorter, and I clearly communicated when their behaviour, particularly towards Andrea, was not acceptable. I spent more time nurturing my friendships, finding solace in the company of those who uplifted me rather than dragged me down. My business, which had been suffering from my divided attention, began to flourish as I channelled my energy into my work, free from the constant familial strife.

My relationship with Andrea became a sanctuary. I realised that to give myself fully to this relationship, I had to let go of the toxic influence of my family's negative behaviour. They never supported our ideas, never wanted to know how our business was going, never came to visit, and never celebrated our achievements.

Even so, letting my family go wasn't easy. There were days filled with guilt and doubt when I wondered if I was making the right choice. Deep down, I believed that I could love my family but still choose to keep them away from my life because their presence was harmful. I had developed enough self-worth to understand this.

As I sat discussing our future with Andrea in the evenings, I felt a sense of peace. The more I reduced contact with my family, the better I started to feel. In turn, my relationship with Andrea grew stronger and closer. I knew I was on the right track. I still felt moments of weakness and sorrow when I would forgive them and increase contact. When the same old negative patterns re-emerged, I realised I was right for cutting them off.

BUILDING YOUR FAMILY DIFFERENTLY

Andrea and his family, our mutual and individual friends, our clients and business partners: these are our chosen family, and we build all these relationships with care. Here are some of the ways we have strengthened ties with our chosen family:

Shared experiences play a crucial role in our family bonds. We create family memories through our daily routine, such as sharing meals, going to gigs and events, and celebrating special occasions like birthdays, holidays and significant milestones.

Mutual support and being there for each other during tough times is all about offering empathy and understanding. We want our family members to feel valued and understood. We offer practical help when we can, fostering a sense of dependability and care. We encourage and support each other, boost everyone's self-esteem, and create a nurturing environment where everyone feels motivated to pursue their dreams.

Effective communication maintains strong family bonds, as I mentioned in the section about the essentials of love. Active listening, where everyone pays close attention to each other's perspectives, fosters mutual respect and understanding. I address disputes with friends, colleagues and Andrea with the same commitment, and find compromises that strengthen our relationships and builds trust.

Establishing traditions creates a sense of identity and continuity. Regular rituals, such as weekly game nights or annual vacations, are fun and something to look forward to. Where it feels right, you might uphold cultural or religious traditions that support your sense of heritage and belonging.

CONCLUSION

In this chapter, I have shared the biggest and most important message of this book: that deep, intimate relationships are built when both partners are 'all in' from the start. I've looked at the various forms and expressions of love, including the 'black t-shirts' (or basics) without which we cannot really thrive in our romantic relationships.

I want you to understand where I am coming from as I share what I have learned from my inner journey, from Andrea and from friends and family.

I have painted a picture for you of the profound influence that Andrea's love has had on my life, and the difficult decisions I have made as I built my self-esteem. We have had the great gift of learning from the clients of our dating agency, Beau Brummell Introductions. Andrea and I have created an extraordinary life and business together, the fulfillment of our dreams thus far. We want to inspire you to find your partner and your expression of love, which is why I have dedicated the entire next chapter to the king of all the skills of love. Can you remember what it is?

CHAPTER TWO

Listening skills

Listening deeply, patiently and actively is the most loving gift you can give your partner, your family and friends, or the person you have just met. Andrea and I have seen over and over how important listening is in our life together and as a way to help our love flourish.

As the ancient Greek mathematician Pythagoras once said, 'A fool is known by speech and a wise man by silence.' Most of us believe we are skilled listeners but few of us (if honest with ourselves) are. We want to make our point. We feel misunderstood. But we also don't know how to listen in a way that makes our partner feel we get them.

Nothing is more attractive than someone listening to you. When you become an expert in listening, you resolve conflicts, deepen understanding, and build lasting respect in every relationship. In this chapter, I will explore listening and its benefits. I will share five ways to enhance your ability to listen that I have found to be helpful in my relationship and explain why they matter.

Listening is not a passive act; it's a skill that requires practice and intention. It is also the key to being engaged in life. When we listen, we open ourselves to deeper connections and empathy.

This skill strengthens relationships, sharpens decision-making, and unlocks opportunities we might otherwise miss. Mastering the art of listening creates a foundation for personal and professional growth, allowing us to reach our highest potential.

THE FIRST LISTENING SKILL: BREATH

Before we can truly listen to anyone or anything around us, we must first learn to listen to our breath. It is the very first rhythm we ever hear – the gentle inhale and exhale that marks the beginning of life. Without breath, we would not be here. And without learning to listen to it, we cannot expect to truly listen to the world, to others or even to ourselves.

Our breath is always speaking to us. It tells us when we're anxious, when we're calm, when we're holding back, or when we are letting go. But most of us move through our days without tuning into this quiet, essential guide. In our noisy, fast-paced world, it's easy to forget that listening doesn't begin with ears – it begins with awareness. And awareness begins with breath.

When we train ourselves to pause and feel our breath – its depth, its speed, its ease or resistance – we are practising the most fundamental kind of listening. It brings us into the present moment. It grounds us. It helps us regulate emotion, centre our thoughts, and create space before reacting. All other listening skills – patience, empathy, presence, comprehension – grow more naturally when our breath is calm and steady.

Listening to our breath teaches us to be still, to be attuned, to wait without rushing in. It's the foundation of all human connection.

If we don't get this one skill right, the rest will be shaky at best. But when we do, we create the conditions for every other listening skill to flourish. So let this chapter begin not with a technique or a checklist, but with something much simpler – and far more powerful: the quiet, steady rhythm of your own breath. Listen to it. Let it lead. Everything else will follow.

LISTENING TO EACH OTHER

It hasn't been easy for Andrea and me to learn to listen to each other. It took time and patience. When Andrea moved to Australia, it was an exciting and challenging time. We were both adjusting to sharing our space, routines and habits. The honeymoon phase gave way to moments of frustration. One day, things boiled over. We ended up shouting at each other over something trivial, a disagreement that spiralled out of control because of the stress we were feeling. At that moment, we both lost our cool, saying things we didn't mean. It was a harsh reminder of how things can escalate when emotions take the lead.

After we had some time to cool down, I realised the core issue wasn't about what we were arguing over; it was about feeling unheard and misunderstood. We sat down and listened to each other. We took turns speaking while the other listened without interrupting. As we talked, I focused on understanding Andrea's perspective, and Andrea did the same for me. By the end of our conversation, we had a much deeper understanding of each other's feelings and needs.

This experience taught us that listening resolves conflict and maintains a strong, healthy relationship. It helped us turn a moment of anger into an opportunity for growth, deepening our connection rather than driving us apart. By giving each other the space to be heard and understood, we moved past the disagreement and built a stronger foundation for our life together. From that point on, we prioritised listening in our relationship. By listening to each other, we express our love.

Over the years, we have become so much better at listening to each other. We are experts in letting the other know he is heard. Of all the skills we have used to maintain our relationship, this has been the single most important one. I could write an entire book about it. We resolve conflicts by listening, and we have built enormous mutual understanding and respect with this one skill.

I am going to show you what Andrea and I have learned. These ideas are the same ones that we share with the hundreds of clients we have worked with in our dating agency over the years. It is the first area we address when clients sign up to find a partner.

'From the first date,' we tell clients, 'You will use your listening skills. You will listen to respect your date, but also to understand whether they are the right person for you. Do they also listen? Or are they only interested in the sound of their own voice? Is there an exchange or a one-way conversation?'

LISTEN IN ALL YOUR RELATIONSHIPS

Strong listening skills enhance intimacy, trust and emotional connections beyond romantic relationships. Listening will help you build stronger friendships and have more satisfying family interactions.

Listening in friendships solidifies trust. When my friends listen to me without judgement, they create a bond between us based on mutual respect and empathy. I feel comfortable sharing my true self, knowing they will meet me with compassion and acceptance. When I feel heard, and I, in turn, listen to my friends, we reinforce trust in the friendship, making us turn more often to each other in times of need.

Your family relationships will also benefit from your strong listening skills. Emotions can run high and family conflicts happen often. Listening is a powerful tool for resolution and understanding.

When family members listen to each other with patience and empathy, it fosters an environment of respect and cooperation. This is important in parent–child relationships, where listening helps children feel valued and understood, promoting their healthy emotional development. For parents, it means being attuned to their children's needs and responding with support and guidance. For siblings, it means establishing a camaraderie that can last a lifetime.

NATURE WALKS WITH MY GRANDMOTHER

I will never forget the lessons my dear grandmother, my mum's mother, taught me as we walked in the woods around my childhood home. I remember with tenderness our walks in the dewy hours of the morning or early evenings. This is where, as a child, I learned the sacred rite of listening, not from my school classroom but from the quiet counsel of my grandmother, a strong woman who had a softer side.

Being silent together made me feel so close to her. She held my hand as we walked, listening to the wind in the leaves. My grandmother would hush me if I tried to chat and help me listen to all the natural sounds around me, the crunching of our feet on the ground, the birds calling as we passed, our breath as we toiled uphill. In the silence, there was a symphony, and we were the audience. From this, I understood: to listen was to learn. This was my first classroom, and nature was the grand instructor, with my grandmother acting as the interpreter.

Our conversations later, over the evening meal, were where we discussed the day's lessons. My grandmother, with her gentle voice, would encourage me to share my thoughts and feelings. These shared reflections were far more than mere dialogue. I felt a sense of communion with my grandmother, despite our age difference. She was a tremendous influence on me. She shaped my future in ways I did not yet understand. She showed me how it felt to be listened to and that is a lesson I have never forgotten. I became a keeper of her legacy, a guardian of the art of listening.

I learned to apply my grandmother's skill even in the chaos of the school playground. When my friends told me their problems, I stayed quiet and listened, like my grandmother had taught me. I noticed how that drew people to me. I even found my parents turning to me for my listening skills, especially my mother. She'd talk to me about her dreams and worries, and I would listen.

In my work, I show my clients how powerful listening is by listening to them. I let them talk without interruption as I get to know them.

The place I am most thankful for my grandmother's lesson is in my romantic relationships. I found my listening skills connected me to my lovers. For some of my partners, my quiet attention was their first experience of deep listening. I loved the connection that it brought, and I showed them how to listen to me. I knew how to tell I was being listened to because I tuned back into how I felt with my grandmother.

BARRIERS TO LISTENING

When Andrea first arrived in Australia, he was full of hope and excitement, ready to embrace a new chapter of his life. However, his thick Italian accent got in the way. On his first day, Andrea noticed the impatience on people's faces when he spoke. His Italian lilt caused irritation and impatience. People cut conversations short and interrupted his explanations.

This communication barrier seeped into our personal life as well. In my experience, the Italians treat conversation as an art form. There are a lot of back-and-forth interruptions that signify engagement and a high level of emotional exchange. People talk over each other, not out of rudeness, but to show their investment in the conversation.

But I grew up in the Croatian culture which, like Australian culture, emphasises waiting for the other person to finish before responding. This clash in communication styles often led to misunderstandings. Andrea would interrupt, thinking he was showing interest, while I saw it as rudeness. When I waited after Andrea spoke to see if he had more to say, Andrea felt a lack of engagement and support.

These differences in listening styles became one of the most significant challenges in our relationship. We had to confront our habits and learn to adapt. I learned to listen to the nuances in Andrea's speech. Andrea learned to slow down, respect the pauses and to give me time to respond.

Recognising these cultural differences was the first step. We both committed to improving our communication, knowing that understanding each other's backgrounds was crucial. Andrea practised patience, while I worked on showing more immediate engagement during conversations.

It was a journey of mutual growth. We read books on communication, attended workshops and had open and honest discussions about our struggles. Andrea shared how it felt to sense people's impatience and the feeling of alienation that came with it. I explained the discomfort of being talked over and the feeling of not being given a chance to contribute.

Through these efforts, we found a middle ground. Andrea's accent became less of a barrier. We learned to appreciate each other's perspectives, blending our cultural differences into a richer, more empathetic way of communicating. We learned that listening was not just about hearing words but understanding the feelings behind them. Patience and a willingness to bridge cultural gaps created a deeper connection and a stronger foundation for our future together.

However, you cannot solve all your relationship problems by being a great listener. Whether in romantic relationships, friendships or family relationships, it takes two to listen. The reasons someone can't listen are many. For example, they may harbour unresolved negative emotions or be dealing with deep-seated trauma. These issues must be addressed.

Why does communication sometimes break down? Here's what I have learned from Andrea and our clients.

Distraction

Your phone keeps buzzing with Instagram notifications while your date talks about their family. Your mind drifts to that work deadline tomorrow instead of focusing on their story about travelling through Europe. You catch yourself people-watching through the window or thinking about what to say next, missing half of what they're sharing. After a long workday, mental exhaustion can make it hard to follow even the most interesting conversation. Dating and relationships in our connected world means fighting against endless distractions that steal attention from the person right in front of you.

Bias

You might decide someone's 'not your type' before really hearing their story. When a date mentions they love something you hate, like horror movies or camping, your brain might switch off. Past relationship hurts can make you jump to conclusions, thinking 'they're just like my ex' before giving them a chance. Their accent reminds you of someone you don't like. They grew up in a different culture, so their way of showing interest looks like disinterest to you. Different communication styles clash, maybe you're direct while they're subtle, leading to misunderstandings. You might take someone less seriously because they're younger or have a high voice.

Negative emotions

Nerves can block real listening; you're so worried about making a good impression that you miss what they're saying. When they mention their ex, a wave of jealousy might hijack your attention. If you're still hurting from a breakup, emotional walls can stop you from truly hearing someone new. Fear of getting hurt again often creates a protective shield that blocks genuine connection.

Environment

A funky restaurant is fun but not great for conversation. If it's so loud you keep asking 'What?' every few minutes, or the coffee shop's espresso machine screams right during the important parts of their story, you don't get far. You might have picked outdoor dining, but now traffic noise drowns out half the conversation. That cramped corner table means you're distracted by servers squeezing past every few minutes.

Difference

He's passionate about cryptocurrency, but your eyes glaze over as he explains blockchain. When he dives deep into his stamp collection, you struggle to show interest. Without shared context about his favourite hobby or field of work, you miss the excitement in his stories. It's okay to be honest (kindly) if you don't share the other person's passions. Look for an interest you do have in common.

Physical

In a dimly lit bar, you miss his subtle smile. After a long day, physical tiredness makes it hard for you to focus on his stories. If you or he has a health issue like hearing problems, anxiety or ADHD, you might find it extra challenging to stay present in the conversation. You decide there's no spark and might mentally check out before really getting to know him.

FIVE WAYS TO HEAR MORE THAN WORDS

Andrea and I have found that listening is more than just hearing each other's words. To make sure each of us feels heard by the other, we practise five ways to listen. While we try our best, we don't always get this right, of course. It takes practice, and sometimes it works well, sometimes we realise we have to try harder.

When Andrea uses the five ways to listen, my trust in him builds as does my sense of rapport. When I feel heard and understood, I am more open, and that builds deeper connections.

In summary, the five ways to hear more than words are:

- Maintain eye contact
- Practise active and reflective listening
- Don't interrupt
- Manage negative emotions
- Minimise distractions

Maintain eye contact
I don't feel heard unless Andrea is looking at me. I don't mean gazing at me, but looking up at me from time to time. When he does this, I feel like he is checking in with how I am responding to his words. I feel seen as well as heard. This simple yet powerful act shows attentiveness and builds trust, signalling to me that my words matter. It is important to strike a balance with eye contact, so that it feels natural rather than intense, to avoid making anyone uncomfortable. Complementing eye contact with nods or smiles can further convey engagement.

Practise active and reflective listening
When you listen 'actively', you create a safe space for your partner to express themselves. What is involved in active listening?

Despite our best efforts, it's easy to misunderstand and be misunderstood. That's why it is helpful to reflect on what the other person has said to you, and in your reply, paraphrase their words and acknowledge their emotions. This way, you show that you have been listening carefully, and you are taking their comments seriously. Reflecting on what Andrea has said and then paraphrasing and repeating it to him ensures I have understood the message. Don't add your own flourishes.

Start your paraphrasing with, 'What I hear you saying is …' Reflect the other person's emotions with comments such as, 'It sounds like you're heartbroken and confused' or 'That sounds challenging; I think I can understand why you're feeling this way.' These conversations can feel awkward, but you will get better with practice.

Don't interrupt
Is there anything more frustrating than someone interrupting you? Practise patience and allow your lover to finish his thoughts before responding. Then encourage him to continue by using words such as, 'I see,' or 'Go on'. If you need to clarify or steer the conversation, ask permission to interrupt. 'Can I interrupt you there, darling? I just want to check that I understand what you are saying.'

Manage negative emotions
Negative emotions, such as anger, fear or blame, run high during times of conflict. When I feel myself getting upset with Andrea, which is rare, I use techniques such as deep breathing, taking a quick break, or acknowledging his feelings and my own without judgement, to calm myself. Saying, 'I can see that this is upsetting for you', can help to de-escalate the situation.

When you manage your emotions, you will be taken seriously in conflict. And you will find a resolution without the risk of outbursts you will regret later.

Minimise distractions
Give your lover your full attention. Turn off electronic devices and choose a quiet, comfortable setting. Make your body language open and inviting, so the other person can concentrate on what he wants to say. When you cross your arms or look away, he may be distracted by worrying about your reactions. Instead, when you lean forward a little to show your interest and attentiveness, you give the other person permission to concentrate on their words. Distractions come from the world around you. I can't tell you how many times I've seen a first date fall flat simply because of the wrong choice of venue, as I discussed in the 'Environment' section above. Picture this: two people finally meet after weeks of anticipation, and they end up in a crowded bar where the music is so loud they can barely hear each other. By the end of the night, both leave frustrated, not because they weren't compatible, but because they never actually got the chance to connect.

That's why the venue matters so much. A first date should be about creating space for conversation, for laughter, for those small pauses when you really see the other person. Somewhere calm and quiet enough that you can hear not just their words, but the tone of their voice, the way they tell a story, the little details that draw you closer.

When Andrea and I first started going on dates, we learned this quickly. One evening we chose a trendy spot that everyone was talking about. It looked great, but we spent half the night leaning across the table shouting 'What?' at each other. By the end, we were more tired than excited. The next time, we kept it simple – a quiet cafe, just the two of us, coffee and dessert. That night, the conversation flowed easily. We left feeling lighter, closer, as though we had really been let into each other's worlds.

So, my advice is simple: choose somewhere that lets *you* be the highlight of the evening, not the noise, not the crowd, not the waiter constantly asking if you want another round. The best first dates happen in places where the only thing competing for attention is the spark between you.

PRACTISE THE FIVE WAYS

The five ways of listening might feel a little stilted at first, and a lot to keep in mind in the heat of the moment. You may even worry that your partner won't think you are sincere. In my experience, there is not much risk of this, but here's a couple of caveats.

Eye contact and body language may have different connotations in different cultures. I am not an expert on this, so here's my tip: if your partner seems uncomfortable with eye contact, ask him why with kindness. For example, 'I've noticed that you prefer to look away when you are talking to me. Are you okay when I look at you directly?'

Also, we have found the need for give and take. If I prioritise someone else's feelings and concerns over my own too often, I feel exhausted. This imbalance creates a dynamic where I feel overwhelmed and unable to assert my needs. Also, when I have my own crises going on and feel stressed, I find it so much harder to listen to others. You may find the same as you start to practise listening. Some days you will be better at it than others.

MORE TOOLS TO HELP YOU LISTEN DEEPLY
Ask open-ended questions
Nothing shuts down a conversation faster than asking questions with a yes/no answer (a closed-end question). I ask Andrea open-ended questions to show I am interested and listening. Giving your partner the opportunity to elaborate may bring vital new information into the conversation.

Open-ended questions can be very broad, such as, 'How are you feeling about everything?' A narrower open-ended question might be, 'What are your thoughts about what I just shared?' Compare this to the closed-ended version: 'Do you agree with what I just said?', which is answered with 'Yes' or 'No'.

Show empathy
I love it when Andrea shows empathy to me by adding expressions of care and concern after paraphrasing what I have said. It doesn't mean he agrees with me, but it shows he cares. Empathy deepens connections and affirms the speaker's feelings. Acknowledge feelings with phrases like: 'I can see why that would make you upset.' Or 'I understand why you feel this way.' You can make such a difference. Non-verbal cues,

such as a comforting touch or matching his facial expression, also conveys your feelings of empathy.

Focus on interests, not positions

When you're in conflict with your partner, it's important to look beneath the surface of the argument. Often, what we're upset about on the outside isn't the real issue – it's just the trigger. The deeper need is usually something more emotional.

For example, you might find yourself snapping about the recycling. On the surface it looks like you're angry about the bins, but underneath, the real frustration might be that you feel like you're carrying the household responsibilities on your own and you'd like more support. The recycling is just the symbol – it's not really about the bins at all.

Or maybe your partner gets annoyed because you're on your phone in the evening. The complaint might sound like 'You're always scrolling', but the deeper message could be, *I miss your attention, I want to feel connected to you.*

When you train yourself to listen for the underlying message, not just the words, you move from arguing about tasks to understanding each other's feelings. And that's where solutions that actually strengthen the relationship come from. If the real need is to feel supported, then sharing responsibilities more fairly will matter much more than who takes out the bins. If the real need is connection, then putting the phone away for half an hour to be fully present will speak louder than any apology.

The heart of it is this: focus less on the 'What' and more on the 'Why'. That's where conflict can turn into closeness.

Provide encouragement
Positive words and body language help de-escalate negative emotions. It shows the other person that you are taking in everything he says. Nod, smile encouragingly and glance up. Say brief affirmations, such as 'Go on', 'Tell me more', and 'I hear you'.

Create an open and safe environment
When Andrea and I know we have a difficult conversation ahead, we find a safe place to talk, where we both feel comfortable expressing our thoughts and feelings. We make sure that we have equal opportunity to speak without being interrupted and give each other our full attention. This encourages honest and open communication between us. Feeling safe also means we can take a step back from our heightened emotions to communicate without feeling afraid of attack.

TRUST IN EVERYTHING: HOW MONEY, BELIEF, AND DREAMS BUILT OUR RELATIONSHIP

When Andrea and I first chose each other, we didn't just fall in love. We made a conscious decision to build a life together completely, courageously, and without safety nets. What we had wasn't the traditional security most couples are told they need before leaping into the unknown. There were no family inheritances waiting for us, no backup savings hidden away, no mapped-out career ladders to climb side-by-side. There was just us. And a belief that love, real, whole, all-in love, would be enough.

Combining our lives and our accounts

From the very beginning, we joined everything we had together. It wasn't much. A modest sum of savings. This was the remains of a year spent keeping our international relationship alive, flying back and forth across countries, across time zones, across the versions of ourselves we had been before meeting each other.

People often underestimate how expensive love can be when oceans separate you. Every visit, every plane ticket, every extended hotel stay chipped away at our finances. But we never measured the cost. Each sacrifice brought us closer to the life we both wanted. From the beginning we were all in.

When we decided to close the distance, neither of us hesitated. We pooled every cent into one shared account, a simple but profound act of faith. This choice was not about convenience. It was about *trust*. It was about saying, with our actions as much as with our words: 'There is no mine or yours anymore. There is only ours.'

The conversations nobody warns you about

There's a truth many couples discover only once they are deep into their relationship: love without trust around money is fragile. Money is never just about dollars or euros or credit card balances. Money touches everything: security, freedom, control, dreams, fears. And unless you talk about it openly, unless you strip away the shame, judgement and assumptions, money can erode even the strongest bonds.

From the beginning, we decided there would be no secrets. We shared both the numbers and the stories behind them. How we felt about spending, saving, giving, risking. What money meant to each of us growing up. What it meant now that we were building something new together.

There were uncomfortable conversations at times. Moments when fear crept in. Moments when old habits whispered, 'Hold something back, just in case.' But every time, we chose honesty over comfort. We trusted each other with everything, not because it was easy, but because it was necessary.

In love, there is no halfway.

Building a dream on four pieces of plastic
If the story ended with two young men, madly in love and financially united, it would be a good one. But this was just the beginning. Soon after joining our lives, we decided to chase an even bigger dream: To build something of our own. A business. A future shaped by our own hands, on our own terms.

We didn't have investors. We didn't have any startup capital. We had four credit cards.

And belief. Endless, stubborn, foolish, magnificent belief.

We maxed out those cards one after another, paying for websites, marketing, first hires, the basic building blocks of what we envisioned. Not because we were reckless but because we were certain.

I sometimes wonder how we kept our nerve. Logic would have told us to slow down. Fear would have insisted we keep one foot on safe ground. But we didn't listen. Not once did we say, 'What if it fails?' The only question we asked ourselves was, 'What will it look like when it works?'

This mindset, this full-hearted commitment, carried us through every challenge. We never let negativity in. We guarded our dream like you would guard a fire in a storm: shielding it from every gust of doubt, feeding it with every scrap of hope.

And slowly, the business grew. The credit cards began to clear. The dream that once existed only between us became real and visible to others, sustainable, thriving.

Lessons money taught us about love
If there's one thing our journey taught us, it's that money will test your love more deeply than almost anything else. It will test your patience. It will test your fears. It will reveal how much you really trust the person standing beside you. Money has the power to separate couples, not because of the number in their bank accounts, but because of the fear behind it. Fear of not having enough. Fear of losing control. Fear of trusting someone else with your future. We didn't escape those fears. We faced them. We disarmed them by doing the one thing fear can't survive: we believed in each other completely.

Today, our relationship with money is still shaped by those early days. We manage it together. We plan together. We take risks together. We win together. And if we ever lose, we lose together, too.

There's no 'mine' and 'yours', only 'ours', always

Trust was always our greatest investment. People sometimes ask us, 'What was the best decision you made?' And they expect an answer about timing, strategy, or some lucky break. But it's none of those things. The best decision we ever made was to trust. Fully. Radically. Without reservation.

Trust was the first seed we planted. Before there was a business. Before there was financial stability. Before there was anything concrete to hold onto.

Trust in each other, in our dream, in the life we were building; that was the soil that allowed everything else to grow. It's still the soil everything grows from today.

In the end, our story isn't about money. It's about faith. It's about two people choosing, again and again, to believe in each other when it would have been easier, safer to doubt. It's about building something real, brick-by-brick, hand-in-hand, fuelled not by certainty, but by love.

And if we could go back and do it all again, we would do it in a heartbeat. The fear, the debt, the sleepless nights, the blind leaps. Because everything we have today was born from that wild, beautiful, all-in trust. And nothing could ever be more valuable than that.

LOVEMAKING AS LISTENING

The listening shared in lovemaking creates a powerful intimate connection that is beyond words if you let it. In the early days of our relationship, Andrea and I often lay together, skin to skin, the hours passing in a comfortable, intimate silence. Night would fall and we'd whisper jokes or spin stories, responding to each other with tenderness.

On our first holiday together, fresco paintings adorned the ceiling above our bed, an expanse of romantic Renaissance imagery. We would point to those images, weaving our own stories into them, or look at each other and smile when words failed us. The frescos became a big part of our sensual experience together. We would look at them, even in the act of love, and say, 'How lucky are we?'

In quiet moments, Andrea would catch me watching him, a silent conversation passing between us. We would lean closer, lips parting and touching, our breaths mingling in the warm air. It was as if our souls became entwined in that silence.

We explored each other, our bodies fitting together. His hand would rest on my tummy to feel the rhythm of my breath, then trail down my leg, making my hips rise to meet his touch. In those moments, we felt like a single being, trembling with a shared desire. Whispering his name, I would hear him echo mine, a sound both calm and eager.

In those profound moments, I knew I would never leave him. He would always be my 'special reason' for everything, the one who listened quietly and understood the language of his touch.

LISTENING AS A PERSONAL JOURNEY AND GROWTH

I was born in 1971, at just five months and ten days' gestation. The strain of my premature birth altered how my parents communicated forever. It was an emotional rupture that was never repaired.

I wasn't a planned baby, and my arrival sparked arguments between my mother and father. What should have been a moment of joy was clouded with fear, strain and resentment. That atmosphere – charged, fragile, and uncertain – was the air I breathed from the very beginning. It left its mark not only on them, but on me. My very existence altered the way they spoke to each other, the way they related, and the way I learned to navigate the world.

Growing up, listening wasn't just something I did – it was a way to survive. I learned to read the subtle cues in people's expressions, their pauses, their shifting body language. I could sense when to stay quiet, when to smile, when to agree, all so I could keep the peace and avoid conflict.

Of course, that also meant I learned how to hide parts of myself. My sexuality, for example, became something I carefully masked. I created connections with people, but often they were surface-level – just enough to belong, but never deep enough to risk rejection. It was a strategy. If I kept things light, if I gave people only what they wanted to see, then I wouldn't have to face their judgement.

At school, it was the same. I listened carefully to my teachers, figured out what they expected of me, and gave it to them. With friends in the playground, I picked my moments, avoiding the situations that could expose me or leave me vulnerable. It was a kind of shapeshifting, a way of adapting so I could keep moving forward without drawing too much attention to the parts of me I was afraid wouldn't be accepted.

Looking back, I can see that my ability to listen and adapt became both my shield and my strength. It protected me when I needed protection, but it also gave me a gift: the skill of really hearing people. Today, that's the same skill I use in my work and in my relationships – the ability to tune into what isn't said, to understand what lies beneath the surface. What once kept me safe has now become one of the greatest tools I carry.

At home, my father's detachment was a constant reminder of the chasm between us. Coupled with my mother's overprotectiveness, this shaped my understanding of familial dynamics. I learned to listen to their fears and motivations. I listened to the silences at the dinner table, the unspoken tensions that hung in the air. I grew to understand that my father's indifference was rooted in his own insecurities and fears, and I felt some compassion and understanding for him.

My escape from the harsh realities of my home was through the companionship of adults. Local architect Josip Duic, who was the son-in-law of my godmother, taught me to paint and draw. Then there was the town drunk, who told me his tales of love and loss. And the elegant Teta Rina Vodopic, a local town woman who shared her meticulously tended garden with me. Each of them imparted lessons that required attentive listening. These interactions nurtured my creativity and provided a sanctuary from the cruelty shown towards me by my peers because I liked flowers and knitting and was a different kind of boy.

From the architect, I learned to see the world through different perspectives and to listen to the stories that buildings and spaces could tell. With the town drunk, I discovered the depth of human experience: the joys and sorrows that define our existence. With the elegant lady, I found beauty in the smallest details, in the patterns of her garden and the grace with which she carried herself.

Later, yoga became a space where I could listen to my body, honour my emotions, and connect with my inner self, a sanctuary. Yoga brought me full circle, teaching me to listen inwardly, embrace my truths and find peace within. Listening to myself became the cornerstone of my survival and growth. I learned to quieten my mind and tune into the whispers of my soul. I discovered the power of breath and the way it could ground me and bring me back to the present moment.

Listening is the thread that weaves through every chapter of my life. It has been my anchor in times of turmoil, my guide in moments of uncertainty, and my source of strength in the face of adversity. Listening has taught me to be present, to be empathetic, and to find beauty everywhere. It has helped me navigate the complexities of my relationship with Andrea and, through our work in BBI, I have found my path, my purpose and my place in the world.

CONCLUSION

A great listener is an irresistible partner. If you find one, hang on to them. If you are one, gently guide your partner to build their listening skills. If you are both great listeners, I wish you a long and deep relationship.

Listening is a skill; you can learn to do it better. The better you get at it, the better all your relationships will be: lovers, friends, family and colleagues. Listening will help solve almost all conflicts and heartache, just as failing to listen will very likely cause heartbreak.

This is important, so I will mention once more that the five most important ways to listen are:

- Maintain eye contact
- Practise active and reflective listening
- Don't interrupt
- Manage negative emotions
- Minimise distractions

Listening in loving relationships is about more than hearing the other person's words; it is about understanding emotions and underlying issues and working together towards a resolution.

CHAPTER THREE

Carnivals and masks

Every year, as I joined in the festivities of the local carnival in my hometown of Kuna Pelješka in Croatia, I imagined a life free of the narrow social expectations I knew would be impossible for me to fulfil. In one such joyous parade, I first got to wear a dress and women's boots!

Carnivals, with their vibrant colours, infectious rhythms, and sense of happiness, are a profound expression of human joy and connection. Thought to have their origins in Roman pagan festivals, carnivals serve as a communal space where social boundaries dissolve, inhibitions fade, and people come together in shared celebration. This atmosphere of revelry and freedom plays a delightful role in fostering and nurturing love.

Carnivals have a special meaning in the gay community. We embrace them. From the first Gay and Lesbian Mardi Gras in Sydney in 1978, we co-opted the carnival for political and social reasons. Here is a place where we get to revel in our differences as queers and express our joy and connection.

The emotions of the carnival, and the masks participants wear, play out in gay relationships in good and bad ways. Emotions gush. The collective joy enhances our sense of belonging, making it easier to form deep connections.

We lower barriers that hinder emotional intimacy and engage with one another more honestly.

The playful spirit of carnivals revives our spontaneity and curiosity – two essential ingredients for romantic attraction. The festive atmosphere invites us to let go of our fears and embrace the moment, welcome the adventure and excitement of new relationships and rekindle the fires of existing ones.

I cannot write a book about gay love and dating without exploring the symbolic and actual roles of the carnival in our culture and history. We have an opportunity here to harness something special in the carnival's age-old role as creator and sustainer of love. And, with some imagination, we can tap into the deeper, darker side of all that carnivals symbolise and use it to better understand our lovers.

THE DUBROVNIK CARNIVAL

One of the most exciting times in my childhood in Croatia, then called Yugoslavia, was during carnival time in Dubrovnik, the coastal town with its famous walls that attract millions of tourists every year. From a young age, I loved the annual trip from Kuna, down the coast to the exciting streets of Dubrovnik, rugged up against the wintery chills of February.

The Dubrovnik carnival is a vibrant collision of past and present. Each year, the town surrenders itself to the ancient rhythms of celebration. In a ceremonial moment when the mayor passes the city keys to the carnival's Master of Ceremonies, something stirs within the cobblestones and the sea air, palpable and thrilling. The masks we wear as part of this carnival represent a shield against the passing shadows of winter, and their painted surfaces conjure forth the youthful vitality of the approaching spring.

Bells echoed throughout our days, played by the *Zvončari* or bell men. These performers, originating in ancient Slavic traditions, were believed to ward off evil spirits with the sound of their bells and the fierce presence of their animal costumes. Their dance was primal, unbridled. As February's frost relented, the great carnival parade began, over 8000 souls adorned in traditional garb for a contemporary masquerade. Floats brought a cavalcade of satire that stitched together global and local events.

Here, in the carnival's embrace, I learned the liberating joy of becoming someone who did not conform to social expectations of gender and sexuality. I felt a power in that transformation, a magic that made my heart race. In our ordinary world, with gender definitions sharp and clear-cut, you were a boy or a girl, destined to walk the well-trodden paths laid out before you. But the carnival allowed us to exist outside that staid, safe pattern. In this atmosphere, our parents allowed and encouraged exploration.

The burning of the *Pust*, an effigy that represented everyone's woes and grievances, marked the end of the carnival. I remember standing there, when I was about seven years old, watching the flames curl around the figure, feeling the weight of my own burdens rise with the smoke. Even now, I think about that fire and the way it burned away more than the effigy. We felt a collective catharsis as we watched the effigy become reduced to embers. The city's keys were given back to the mayor and the carnival flag was lowered. Dubrovnik returned to its rhythms. Dull, but marked by the spirit of the festival.

I was part of a small-town community where every face was familiar and every story known. But in the carnival's realm, we became part of something bigger, a world of freedom where the only truth was the one we created.

I still remember my costumes, nothing more elaborate than my mother's dresses and wigs, makeup and high heels, in particular, a pair of red boots that I cherished above all else. I wore them, not with a sense of transgression but of homecoming, a celebration of something unspoken within me.

In those moments, every gay man, and perhaps every person seeking refuge in the anonymity of a mask, discovers a new facet of their being. Not hiding; I was exploring a new side of myself. Reflecting upon those days, I see how those carnivals posed the question, 'What if the roles we assume in the carnivals of life became as fluid and as liberating as the ones we don behind the mask?'

Carnivals are a mirror we hold up to our lives. They reflect our myriad roles and the countless masks we wear daily. In the carnival of life, we are both spectators and performers, our stories shared and interwoven. In remembering and retelling, we keep the spirit of carnivals alive, reminding us that beneath whatever mask we wear, the essence of who we are waits for the moment we choose to reveal it to the world.

Behind every mask worn in the carnival is a secret jubilation that speaks to the truths we seldom voice. For many, especially within the gay community, the mask is more than an accessory: it is a key to a door kept shut. It whispers, 'What might you find if you were not bound by the rigid lines drawn around you?'

LEARNING TO BE WHATEVER YOU WANT

When I was a boy, each carnival brought with it a sense of becoming. Within the folds of a gown and the stiletto of Mum's red boots, I found the space to dream, to wonder what I could embody beyond the script of gender and expectation. I could be anything – a figure of grace and beauty or a creature wild and untamed.

But my transformation was not without trepidation. Taking on a new persona, I felt the fear of the unknown. This fear made the carnival's call irresistible. It was a chance to test the waters, to hear the cadence of an unfamiliar voice rising from my throat, to feel the unfamiliar sway of a body reinvented by imagination. Behind the mask, I could experiment with the contours of my identity and play with my notion of self. The magic of the carnivals lay in its impermanence.

Children are the carnival's truest disciples. Without pretence or the weight of a lifetime's baggage, they teach us to embrace a sense of play unencumbered by judgement. Adults with their critical eyes and guarded hearts could stand to learn from them and let the simple joy override the compulsion to critique and categorise. Children remind us of who we once were, happily living in each moment.

The paradox of our human condition is that the masks we choose to wear, for fun or for fear, both conceal and reveal us. They hide our vulnerabilities, yet they also unveil our longing for freedom.

As the music of the carnival fades into memory, we're left with a warmth that lingers in the soul. It's a reminder of the masks we wore, the laughter we shared, and the silent vows we made to ourselves under the cover of masquerade. The carnival ends, but its spirit continues, urging us to recall the child within us, and to dream of a world where we can all dance freely, unmasked.

In life, we assume masks out of necessity or desire, a leader stepping into their role, a lover adopting vulnerability or an artist wearing the shroud of their muse. Each mask serves its purpose, the freedom it affords or steals away.

The mask we wear for the world is necessary, yet within the sanctity of trust, it must fall away. In its removal lies the pathway to genuine connection. Knowing and loving another is to invite them to remove their masks and reveal the true soul beneath. Whether they choose to do so, how often and how completely is part of the dance.

We are performers in the grandest carnivals of all: life itself. With each new situation, a different aspect of ourselves comes to the fore. Within each of us lives a multitude of characters awaiting the right stage, the perfect moment to emerge. Each encounter shapes and reshapes our existence.

The freedom of the masks is their impermanence – their ability to be put on and taken off. Our true selves, the versions that our partners and close friends cherish, are often obscured beneath the armour we wear to face the world. The roles of 'CEO', 'doctor' and 'business owner' are costumes donned for performance. Our goal is to connect with the essence that lies beneath the layers of titles and expectations.

At work and in love, we find our masks both necessary and burdensome. In work, we strive to balance the mask of professionalism with the human underneath. To fall in love is to lower our guard, remove the mask, and let another see us.

Andrea's and my journey together has been a celebration of unmasking, of finding joy in each other's truest selves. It is the joy that sustains us, that weaves through our days and lifts us above the ordinary. In each other, we find the freedom of the carnivals sustained, a dance of authenticity and play.

THE JOY OF MASKS

Our dear friend's baby shower was approaching. Baby showers are usually reserved for women and children. Andrea had never attended one; had never heard of the concept. For me, it was a reminder of a barrier I knew well, where my presence at such events had raised the unspoken question, 'Why are you here?' The division of genders, for sports, for education, for celebrations like these, seemed forced, a dictate rather than a choice.

When Andrea and I voiced our hesitation about coming, the host and mother-to-be, Jodie, proposed an audacious solution. 'Come in drag,' she declared. In her challenge, there was an unspoken permission to turn the day on its head. We conceived the personas of Ms January and Ms April, our female alter-egos. As we prepared, a sense of anticipation bubbled within us. Donning our over-the-top attire, we stepped into a new realm of freedom.

A kaleidoscope of emotion met our entrance on the day. Some children clung to their mothers, wary of the tall, flamboyant strangers. Some mothers observed us with fear, some with fascination, and some with warmth.

As much as we challenged gender norms that day, we ourselves fell into a gender trap. We mistook one child for a boy because of her navy-striped t-shirt and short haircut. (We are all products of our conditioning.)

We corrected our mistake and the connection with that child became a big part of the day. With the slightest of gestures, a wink, a smile, a subtle exchange of looks, we wove a silent narrative with that child, an understanding that transcended words. By the afternoon's end, we had formed a silent companionship with her, revealed by her small parting kiss on our cheeks, a gesture of kinship. Andrea gifted her a token, a tiny pink cocktail umbrella, a symbol of a newfound freedom to explore all the shades of her being. The mother was astonished at her daughter's uncharacteristic embrace of something so feminine.

Our final act was the most telling that day. Slipping away, Andrea and I shed our disguises to re-emerge as our true selves. The look of recognition, then surprise, on our new child friend's face spoke volumes of the day's impact. It was a lesson for all of us about identity and acceptance. The joy we witnessed in that child, who embraced the day with open arms and an open heart, was a stark contrast to the judgement we so often encounter from the adult world.

The masks we wear, whether for work, protection or play, serve as both barriers and gateways. Like our drag, suits in the corporate world are armour and titles are shields. Masked, we manoeuvre through a maze of expectations and performances. But there comes a point when the mask must come off, when the person beneath must be seen and understood.

Our venture into the world of drag at the baby shower was not just an act of entertainment, but a study in humanity. It was a way to experience and express the multiplicities within us, to challenge the perceptions of others and to change a life, even in the smallest of ways.

When Andrea and I left the event, we carried with us the knowledge that our presence as drag performers had been more than just fun. It was our opportunity to show a richer tapestry of our identities and to show the power of empathy and connection. In that shared space, we found joy, laughter and the purest form of acceptance, from a child who saw past the fabric and makeup to the hearts beneath.

STEPPING OUT FROM THE MASK

Masks are powerful. They let us step into new versions of ourselves and slip into roles we might not otherwise dare to try. But they can also become a way to hide and avoid the hard work of knowing ourselves, and letting others know us, too.

I've seen that. I've lived it. The carnival's energy, the wild freedom of it all, can make you believe you're untouchable. You get caught up in the moment, swept away in the music, the costumes, the delicious rush of being someone else for a night. And sometimes, that means doing things you wouldn't normally do, things that feel exhilarating at the time but leave you empty the next day. A kiss that meant nothing. A connection that became awkward with the dawn. A moment of recklessness that caused real harm.

When masks become a habit, a way of moving through the world without ever being seen, we see their shadow side. When you're used to hiding, when you've spent years learning to blend in, it's easy to forget how to stand bare and be loved for who you truly are. You start wondering: *If they saw me, really saw me, would they still want me?*

And that's the real risk. Not just the superficiality of carnival nights, but the slow erosion of self-worth. The fear that the mask is all that makes you interesting, desirable, worthy of attention. It's a seductive lie, and it can keep you running in circles, chasing highs instead of building something real.

I've been lucky. With Andrea, I found someone who sees me, even when I try to disappear behind a mask. Together, Andrea and I discovered that our masks, worn out of necessity or choice, aren't just about concealment but are also about discovery and expression. We've found in each other a shared joy in our true selves, a journey beyond the facades in previous acts of our lives. Our adventures together and the shedding of past masks have allowed us to find in each other the freedom that once the carnival alone could provide.

Our society is draped in illusion, from the manipulated images in our magazines to the altered personas we encounter in our digital play. The line between the real and the artificial grows tenuous, challenging us to remain anchored in who we truly are. In this world, the mask becomes a tool not just for concealment but also for self-exploration.

The characters we embody in our professions and the roles we play in social settings are masks too, ones that we wear to interact with a world that often demands a performance. The challenge lies in ensuring these masks do not become our faces and that we do not lose ourselves to the characters we portray.

Each mask we wear, from those our society hands us to the ones we select for ourselves, shapes our identity in subtle ways, yet the unmasking reveals our humanity, the laughter, the tears, the raw edges and the smooth contours of our individuality.

The most profound courage lies in laying down the mask, being vulnerable and allowing our true selves to be seen and known. In this, we find genuine connection and encounter love not just as an emotion but as an act of bravery. Genuine relationships are born from this place of openness. They thrive not on the masks we wear but on the faces we reveal. In Andrea, I have found both the mirror and the window, a reflection of my true self and a vista into a world where togetherness means being unafraid to be unmasked.

The art of living is much like the art of the carnival. It is about finding balance – knowing when to don the mask for the show and when to remove it for the soul. Always remember, amidst the charades and the masquerades, to remain true to yourself, for in that truth lies the path to genuine joy and unbounded freedom.

CONCLUSION

The carnival was never just a festival for me; it was an unveiling. It revealed the hidden, the possible, the joyous truth beneath the everyday disguises we wear. It was where I first glimpsed the full spectrum of who I could be. And it was where I learned that love, true love, thrives not in the masks we craft but when we show the courage to remove them.

Yes, we move through life donning different faces, playing the roles demanded of us, adjusting our performance to suit the stage. Some masks protect us; others imprison us. In love, as in the carnival, we are both the spectacle and the spectator. We can play and have fun. But love demands something more at times. It invites us to step beyond the performance and risk being seen, to trust that we are enough without the disguise.

Carnivals, at their heart, remind us of the joy in transformation, but also of the greater joy in returning to ourselves. The thrill of a new persona, the exhilaration of escape, all fade with the final note of music, the last embers of the carnival's ritual fires. What remains is what has always been waiting beneath the unmasked self.

For Andrea and me, love is a dance of revelation. It is in the quiet moments, when he reaches for my hand in an unfamiliar crowd or we laugh over something only we understand, that I feel our masks slip away. Love, I realise, is not just about who we are when we perform, but who we become when we no longer feel the need to perform. Each step is a stripping away of the unnecessary, a movement towards the essential. The carnival taught me how to play and take on a world of possibilities. Love taught me something deeper: how to stay, how to stand bare before Andrea and be known.

And in that knowing, I find something greater than the spectacle, greater than the fleeting magic of a masquerade. I find home.

CHAPTER FOUR

Love and connection

I want you to hear from Andrea, so I invited him to write the first part of this chapter. He writes with honesty about how we built the love and connection between each other.

ANDREA'S STORY

My relationship with Vinko is built on three foundations: trust, respect and communication. We have come to believe that love cannot survive without these foundations and want to share how we strengthened them and what threatened them. The first few months of any relationship are important for creating strong bonds and having open conversations that are deep and meaningful. Vinko has written beautifully about communication in Chapter 2, 'Listening skills'. In this chapter, I address the other two foundations: trust and respect.

After meeting in Dubrovnik, Croatia, Vinko and I returned to Puglia, Italy (my birthplace) to decide our future. Would there be a future, or had our encounter at Dubrovnik been a holiday romance?

Both Vinko and I are emotional, sensitive, family-oriented men, so I had a strong feeling that our stay in Puglia would have a profound effect on us and our future together. As you can imagine, I was both nervous and excited.

As my plane descended from the freezing cold Vienna winter into the warmer climes of Bari, the capital of Puglia, I watched the landscape unfold beneath me, fields of ancient olive trees interspersed with patches of vineyards, all bordered by the drystone walls that are a hallmark of Puglia and of my childhood. It is one of my favourite views. This was more than just a journey home; it was a test of my future relationship with Vinko.

I had left Italy years ago for a life in Austria, building a career in the creative world of architecture, a career that often felt as cold as the northern European weather. But Puglia, with its warm breezes and even warmer people, still called to me. Planning this trip had been a whirlwind of excitement and anxiety. As well as a reunion with Vinko, it was a homecoming for my friend's wedding, an event infused with love and tradition. It was an opportunity to introduce Vinko to my world, to share my childhood memories, my roots and the essence of who I am.

Vinko, on the other hand, made the long journey from Australia, where the landscapes were as open and rugged as Puglia. His arrival in Italy was marked by a mix of exhilaration and apprehension. He knew the significance of this trip; it was not just about exploring a new place but about exploring the depths of our relationship. Would the fertile grounds of Puglia nurture our budding connection, or would the realities of my world pull us apart?

Our reunion was a scene of heartfelt embraces and whispers of relief. The next day, we drove through a part of the countryside where I knew every stone and corner. The car filled with the scent of wild herbs carried on the breeze. The soft murmur of Italian music played in the background, prompting me to sing my favourite songs aloud. I pointed out landmarks and shared snippets of childhood memories, each a big part of my identity.

For me, the anticipation of meeting my family and attending the wedding added layers of nervous energy to my interactions. For Vinko, life in Italy was uncharted territory. Every meal, every stroll through the village streets and every conversation laden with rapid-fire Italian tested his resolve. Could his desire to build a life with me, no matter how strong, withstand the pressures of being in unfamiliar places, not speaking the language and immersion into my strong Italian roots?

Of course, I had made sure there was more to our time together than my time with family and formalities. I had planned private escapes for us to enjoy alone: early morning walks through olive groves, lazy afternoons on secluded beaches and evenings sipping local wine under the stars. On these occasions, we relaxed into each other's company. We talked openly about our dreams and fears, the possibility of a shared future and the challenges of melding our very different lives. These conversations, though difficult and sometimes a bit scary, started building our foundations of trust and respect. Vinko was honest with me about the problems he foresaw and the feelings he struggled with. And so was I. And still we stayed together and showed up to the family events as well as the indulgences.

And Puglia, with its earthy sensuality, amplified the sexual energy between us. Vinko's visit to the land that had shaped me felt profoundly intimate. Now that land witnessed the deepening of our bond. Each touch, each kiss was charged with promise of continuity and growth.

Our trust in each other grew as we navigated the cultural nuances, the unspoken rules of family dynamics, and the sheer effort of managing bilingual conversations. All put our patience and commitment to the test. But we learned to support each other through the missteps and misunderstandings and to adapt to and embrace each other's worlds.

When faced with challenges, we stood together, combined our different backgrounds and complemented one another. I felt a huge amount of respect for Vinko when he did this. The trip to Puglia solidified our relationship.

During our trip, Vinko and I often found ourselves walking for hours down many narrow paths, some lined with fig trees and others with houses or shops. On these walks, we delved deeper into our histories, our dreams and the revelations that had brought us to this precipice of change. Here, I found the courage to reveal my vulnerabilities. I spoke of my partner at the time. Even though he was the kindest person I have ever known and had been in a relationship with, I just lost myself, my true self within the dynamic of this relationship. Vinko listened and told me his heart ached with recognition. He, too, had known the comfort of predictability and the seductive ease of a life unchallenged. He felt his relationship back in Australia had morphed into a routine that numbed more than it nurtured.

As we walked from the protective shade of olive groves to the rugged cliffs that faced the sea, the landscape around us seemed to echo our journey. From safety to something wild.

We discussed the fear of unravelling the ties that bound us to our pasts, not just relationships but the identities we had woven around ourselves. Yet, as the days passed, a shared strength emerged: a mutual resolve to not just exist but to thrive.

We had dinner one evening in Ostuni, known as the white city because of its white-washed houses. It glowed under a crescent moon that night. Our table was in a quiet corner of a terrace draped with bougainvillea in bloom. With each course, we revealed more of ourselves to each other. Vinko's laughter filled the evening air. Later, walking hand-in-hand back to our villa, we stopped and sat under an ancient olive tree that had become a favourite, a silent witness to centuries of change.

It was here that we pledged to a life of togetherness. 'We can do this,' I said, my voice steady. 'Not just survive, but flourish. Together, we can redefine what it means to be free, to be truly ourselves. There is no turning back.'

Vinko reached for my hand. 'With you, I feel like I'm coming home,' he replied.

We talked late into the night of a life where each of us could be our true selves, not shaped by the other but supported, a relationship where growth was not just possible but encouraged … inevitable.

By the time Vinko and I returned from Puglia, we had changed more than our relationship status. We had changed our souls. We had ventured into the uncertainty of new beginnings.

As we met and passed each challenge, we fortified our shared certainty in each other. We found the strength to reclaim our lives. In the rustic beauty of my homeland, we had discovered a future together, rich with possibility and the promise of growth.

We knew we had forged a special connection there among the warm breezes, the ancient olives, and the white-washed houses of Puglia. But perhaps we did not know how special that connection was back then. It wasn't until much later, after we started BBI, after I moved to Sydney Australia, and after Vinko eventually revealed his HIV status to me, that I fully realised how solid those foundations were.

Upon the foundations of trust and respect, our commitment to be honest with each other, and our courage to believe in our love and ability to grow, we have built businesses, friendships, lives and love. And, to our enormous satisfaction, we have helped many other men find their way into strong, deep and loving relationships.

THE THREAD OF TRUST

Trust is an invisible thread that binds people together. It creates connection. Trust allows you to feel safe and secure in your partner's presence. You build trust over time, from the first moment you meet. When you trust someone, you open your heart and mind to them and embrace vulnerability. Your vulnerability creates intimacy.

Trust is also fragile. For Vinko and me, experiences of betrayal and disappointment made it difficult to trust each other sometimes. We found ourselves questioning each other's motives, fearing that history would repeat itself.

Overcoming the fears that stand in the way of trust is about learning to distinguish between past hurts and present possibilities. When you decide to trust someone new, you take a leap of faith and know that with every risk, there is the potential reward of deeper intimacy.

So, there are two steps to strengthen the invisible thread: building trust and overcoming your fears of betrayal.

The basics of trust

Trust builds when you are consistent, honest and reliable. As you can see from my story of our early days, being reliable is a big part of building trust. That means showing up when you say you will, keeping promises, and being honest about your feelings. That establishes a solid foundation of trust.

It starts with self-awareness and a genuine desire to connect on a deeper level. Reflect on your past relationships and identify patterns that have hindered your ability to trust, respect and communicate effectively. Work on healing these wounds and developing healthier habits. Seek out resources, such as books, therapy and workshops, that can provide guidance and support.

RESPECT MEANS VALUE

Mutual respect means that you value your partner. You appreciate his thoughts, feelings and boundaries, and show your respect by acting with kindness and consideration.

Respect does not mean agreeing with everything; it is about acknowledging the differences between you and your partner and valuing them.

Of course, no-one is perfect. Misunderstandings, or a perceived power imbalance, can undermine respect and trust. The way Vinko and I respond is to address any feelings of disrespect directly, constructively and immediately. It's not as hard as it can seem. Just listening to each other's concerns (see Chapter 2) and showing empathy builds respect. When you are willing to listen, you encourage your partner to share their needs and set clear boundaries, which helps prevent misunderstandings.

On our return journey from Italy, both Vinko and I fell into quiet contemplation, facing the realities we had left behind and what was ahead. For me, the transition from the romantic haze of our time together to the everyday rhythms of our separate lives was a delicate dance of joy and a source of trepidation.

When both of us had returned to our respective homes, in our respective countries, our newfound connection felt grounding and also fraught. We had professional and personal commitments; we had not yet broken from our existing relationships.

While Vinko and I spoke about our mutual commitment to this new beginning, the responsibilities of our separate lives loomed large. His then partner deserved honesty and respect. The thought of causing pain to someone he cared about was a heavy burden that clouded his happiness. My situation was also complex. My life in Austria was now suffused with the realisation of what truly mattered. The conversation

I needed to have with my then partner was one of the hardest I'd ever faced.

Navigating this emotional time required the same sincerity and openness that had characterised our initial connection. We discussed our situations with a maturity born of genuine love and respect for all involved. Phone calls became our lifeline, each conversation a step towards resolving the tangled threads of our respective lives.

Vinko's partner had sensed growing distancing between them over recent years that neither man had found the words to address, until now. In the weeks that followed, Vinko and I found the strength to have these difficult conversations and supported each other. Although we celebrated our newfound freedom, we mourned the end of significant chapters in our lives and leaving the people who had mattered so much to us. It was a time of profound growth and painful farewells, a dual process of healing and hurting.

Sometimes, committing to your man means having to let go. Ending these relationships with care and respect taught us that love is not just about joyous moments but also about the difficult decisions. Respect extends to past bonds as well as new ones. We found solace in our shared vision of the future. Building a life with Vinko was both exhilarating and daunting. With his unwavering love and support, I found the courage to embrace the unknown. 'I want us to plant roots in Australia, Croatia and Puglia,' I confessed. 'I want to wake up each morning to the sound of birdsong and the scent of freshly baked bread wherever we are. I want us to have our own olive trees to nurture as we grow old.'

Vinko replied, 'And I want to share in your dreams, Andrea. I want us to build a life filled with joy and laughter, surrounded by the people we love. I want our home to be a sanctuary, a place where we can find refuge from the storms of life.'

We planned a life together, a home filled with laughter where honesty ruled, and we valued difficult conversations as much as declarations of love. We talked openly about a home where our families were welcome and where we could celebrate our lives.

We knew we were embarking on a journey that would shape our lives forever. Together, we would plant the seeds of our dreams and watch them grow, nourished by the trust, love and devotion that bound us together. We knew that the road ahead would be filled with challenges and obstacles, but we also knew that if we had each other, we could weather any storm. Together, we could conquer the world.

We each travelled to the other's homes over this transition time, I to Australia and he to Vienna. We filled these reunions with moments of togetherness. We discovered a language that transcended words, desire that spoke volumes about the depth of our connection. As we lay entwined in each other's arms, the boundaries between us melted away, leaving only the raw intensity of our passion and the unspoken promise of a love that knew no bounds.

The freedom to express myself fully in Vinko's embrace was nothing short of revelatory. Gone were the days of hiding behind closed doors, of suppressing my true desires. With Vinko, I found a partner who accepted me for who I was and embraced every aspect of my being. In his touch, I found comfort and strength, a refuge from the outside world where I could be my truest self.

Vinko also felt the power of our physical and sexual connection. In my arms, he found a sense of belonging he had not known before, a home where his desires were acknowledged and celebrated. He felt a sense of liberation, a freedom from his past that propelled him towards a future filled with endless possibilities. With me, he could be vulnerable and exposed, his deepest desires laid bare without shame or embarrassment.

We knew that our love was destined to endure. It felt like a flame that would burn brightly for all eternity, lighting the way forward on our journey of discovery and desire. However, we were also acutely aware of the challenges that lay ahead. We found the strength to face these obstacles in the knowledge that our love was a force to be reckoned with. This was not just the beginning of a new chapter. It was the start of a grand adventure, a journey of love and discovery that would span the breadth of our lives.

And we turned out to be right. We went all in on our love, and we found what we believed to be possible. We made it possible.

If only that olive tree could talk …

VINKO'S STORY

Once I met Andrea and discovered just how powerful a romantic connection could be, I wanted to share my revelation with other men. That desire was the genesis of Beau Brummell Introductions, our dating service for gay men. The story of how it started is closely woven into our love story and our 'all in' approach to love. Connections have become my life and work.

From the moment we met, we understood that real connections, the kind that fortify the soul and withstand the storms of life, are spun from communication, respect and trust. But for me, as I have written in Chapter 2, listening is where connection is created. Listening is the act of opening not just our ears but our hearts to the rhythm of another person's thoughts, fears, joys and dreams. Developing this skill supported our connection into a long-lasting love.

As society increasingly entrusts relationships to the algorithms of dating apps and social platforms, we put these connections at risk. The swipe of a screen may introduce two souls, but laughing together, sharing a tear, and understanding life's oddities deepens these bonds beyond the superficial.

I recently read some chilling statistics about modern connection. Despite our current generations being the most connected by technology ever, they are also the loneliest. Andrea and I believe the rise in digital dependency is a clarion call to foster genuine connections. BBI quickly became our crusade against the superficial bonds technology encourages. We saw so many men who bailed on their relationships at the first challenge and went back to swiping through the apps in search of perfection, or perhaps others willing to keep things at a surface level.

Our philosophy is that true connection feeds the soul, much like a nourishing meal satisfies the body. Digital interactions leave us craving more because they lack the essential nutrients of genuine human interaction.

Our approach is revolutionary yet simple, something new in today's world, but something ancient too. We insist on meeting our clients. Those personal interactions mean we understand our clients' quirky, mundane and profound dimensions. We believe that in many ways we are like the matchmakers of old, who existed for centuries in many different cultures and communities. We are not in the business of transactions but of transformations. Real love isn't found in the sterile data of profiles but in the messy, beautiful chaos of human interaction. We turn solitary souls into symphonies of shared experiences.

Our formula is to replace algorithms with empathy and understanding, replace profiles with personalities, and trade digital messages for deep conversations.

We create environments where people can meet to listen to each other in a way that words are both spoken and felt. For us, listening is an active, dynamic form of presence and connection. The skill is knowing when to hold silence and when to fill it, how to read the unspoken worries knitting the brow, and how to answer not just the question posed but also the ones hidden in the tremor of the voice.

We found our approach deeply resonated with many men who were frustrated with the hollow promises of online dating and nonplussed about how to get around it. Our clients are often busy men, with full lives, who are open to guidance about how to make and deepen a connection. They yearn for the warmth of human touch, the complexity of human emotion and the beautiful imperfections that make each of us uniquely lovable.

We offer our clients an opportunity to help the world to restore love and connection, trust, respect and communication to their rightful place.

You can do this too. In a world teeming with wires, you can be the thread of trust. In the age of loneliness, you can be the listener. In the realm of fleeting glances, be the gaze that lingers. In the simplicity of true connection lies the blueprint of lasting love.

When we started BBI, we both left our jobs. We had never imagined starting a dating agency but were so thrilled about our relationship that we wanted to share the joy. This was us throwing ourselves all in and building trust. Within two months, we had 19 clients and started matching. This increased to taking 30 clients a month and we hit 400 clients within 12 months. The response amazed us. We had found our people. Others were with us.

FIND A BIGGER PURPOSE TO FORTIFY YOUR LOVE

Creating BBI strengthened the connection between Andrea and me. We recommend that you consider creating a shared project that fortifies your relationship and connection. For you, it might be building a home, playing tennis, travelling or playing bridge. It's not the nature of the project that's important, it's the bond and togetherness. It might be something that you are building and perhaps even fighting for together.

Having a shared project means you will learn so much, and every dispute will deepen your intimacy if you listen. Maybe you prefer to keep your life separate. You must do whatever feels right. Trust your gut. But consider it first.

This is why so many people fall in love with their work mates. Think about times when you have worked on a shared project with anyone – colleague, friend or family. Is that something you enjoy and would like to take into your relationship? If you have never done a project with anyone before, try doing a simple project with someone that doesn't put too much financial strain on you.

CONCLUSION

In this chapter, you have heard from both of us. Andrea shared his story of building respect and trust. I've shared how that influenced our decision to start Beau Brummell Introductions.

Puglia, a land steeped in history and tradition, tested the strength of our relationship and ultimately fortified it. We discovered profound depths of trust, mutual respect and effective communication that transformed our connection into a deeply meaningful and resilient 'all-in' relationship. We celebrated our differences and learned to navigate the cultural nuances that caused friction. We built a foundation that allows our love to flourish and encouraged many others to follow in our footsteps.

Trust allows us to be open and vulnerable, fostering true intimacy. Mutual respect ensures that we both feel valued and understood, creating a balanced partnership. Effective communication bridges the gaps between us, allowing us to share our inner worlds and build a shared understanding.

Through our story, we hope to inspire others to invest in the fundamentals of trust, respect and communication, which lead to deeper, more fulfilling connections that stand the test of time.

CHAPTER FIVE

Self-hatred

Homophobia isn't always obvious or violent. At its core, it's the belief that being gay is less valid, less worthy than being heterosexual, and that belief seeps into everyday interactions. Whether it's a dismissive comment at work, rejection in your family of origin, or the cold shoulder at a shop counter, homophobia shows up as a lack of care at best, and hatred and violence at worst.

Absence of social empathy has real consequences for the Queer community. It fosters shame, depression and even self-hatred. When we've been told for so long that something about us is wrong, those messages take root.

When you are dating and forming relationships, these internal struggles don't disappear, in fact, they become clearer. The way the world treats you shapes how you see yourself. Acknowledging that impact is a crucial part of building intimacy that is real, mutual and grounded in self-worth.

Andrea and I understand how damaging these internal struggles can be. That's why we put empathy, connection and self-worth at the centre of everything we do.

HOW SELF-HATRED MANIFESTS

I don't think anyone sets out to hate themselves. It's something that slowly seeps in, like water through cracks, when the world around you reflects only rejection or shame.

I remember what it felt like when I first realised I was different. Being gay wasn't something I could talk about at home, not in the kind of family I grew up in. The silence alone was heavy, but when silence turned into rejection, it carved something deep inside me. Parents, siblings, people you love the most, when they respond with criticism, coldness, or worse, when they refuse to see you at all, you start to wonder if maybe they're right. Maybe you are unworthy. Maybe there is something wrong with you.

That's the trap of self-hatred: it isn't born in us; it's handed to us. We absorb it from the way others look at us, the words they throw at us, the doors they close in our faces. As a child, I didn't have the tools to push back. So instead, I turned those voices inward. I repeated them until they became my own, until I could hardly tell the difference between their rejection and my own inner critic.

Looking back now, I see it so clearly. That self-hatred never really belonged to me. It was a reflection of their fears, their lack of understanding, their inability to love freely. But at the time, I couldn't see it that way. At the time, it felt like truth.

That's why I always remind people: if you've ever carried that heavy burden, know it isn't yours to keep. The feelings of shame, the belief that you are somehow less – they didn't start with you. And because they didn't start with you, they don't have to stay with you.

We see self-hatred manifest in three ways in ourselves and our clients: negative self-talk, avoidant behaviours and destructive actions.

If you ever notice yourself using harsh or belittling language about yourself – words you would never say to someone else – that's a sign of self-sabotage. For example, thoughts like: *I'm not good enough for them,* or *I'll never find love because of who I am* are clear markers of internalised shame.

Avoidant behaviours are just as damaging. These might include ghosting someone you like because you're afraid they'll reject you first. Or cancelling dates because deep down, you don't believe you're worth someone else's time. It's pulling away before anything real starts, not because you don't want a connection, but because you're scared of what might happen if you try.

Destructive actions can be obvious or subtle. Perhaps you hook up with people who mistreat you because you think that's what you deserve. Or you pick fights, criticise your date, or sabotage a promising relationship just to protect yourself from getting hurt. It seems like self-protection when it's happening, but in the long run, it reinforces the belief that you're unlovable.

Noticing these patterns is the first step. Pause and ask yourself: *Where is this coming from? What am I afraid of?* Being curious about your reactions gives you the power to change them.

As matchmakers, Andrea and I have seen how self-love and self-compassion shape the quality of someone's relationships.

When you believe you're worthy of love, you make space for healthier, more fulfilling connections to grow.

DATING APPS DON'T HELP

In today's world of dating apps and online profiles, these issues are intensified. Dating apps focus on appearance and surface traits, which feed feelings of doubt and insecurity. If you are questioning your worth, the constant comparison to polished profiles wears you down.

Internalised homophobia erodes self-esteem. It leads to harsh self-talk and the belief that you're not good enough. That mindset makes it harder to date or enter a relationship with any sense of ease.

THE WAY FORWARD

Moving forward with strength begins by looking back. That sounds counterintuitive, especially if the past includes pain, trauma, or loss. But when those experiences shape how we see ourselves or how we connect with others, facing them is the only way to loosen their grip.

This means forgiving yourself for past mistakes or recognising that your trauma doesn't define you. It means reflecting on a painful breakup and understanding that it doesn't mean you're unlovable. The work of healing is difficult, but it is necessary. And you don't have to do it alone. There's no shame in seeking professional support if that's what you need.

If you want to show compassion to someone you're dating or in a relationship with, start by showing compassion to yourself.

One place to begin is with your inner voice. For every negative thing you say to yourself, try offering two positives in return. For example, if your mind says, *I always mess things up on dates,* respond with, *I'm a great conversationalist,* and *People appreciate my honesty.* Rethinking your inner narrative in this way takes practice, but over time, it shifts how you relate to yourself, and by extension, to others.

Avoidant behaviours also deserve attention. The antidote to cancelling dates, withdrawing when someone gets too close, or convincing yourself you're 'too busy' for love is to lean in. Instead of avoiding, take one small action, show up for a low-pressure coffee, send a message explaining your state of mind, or agree to a call even if you're unsure. Connection grows from honesty, not perfection.

Destructive actions, such as lashing out, choosing partners who mistreat you, or sabotaging good things before they start, reinforce the very fears you want to escape. The antidote is learning to pause. When triggered or overwhelmed, ask yourself: *What's happening here? Am I reacting to this moment, or to something old and unresolved?* Write it down, go for a walk, or speak with a friend. Break the impulse to act in ways that hurt you or others.

Each of these practices, such as self-kindness, brave connection, and conscious pausing, helps untangle the roots of self-hatred. And each one is a step towards building relationships that are grounded in trust, care, and self-worth.

ROBERT'S STORY: REBUILDING CONNECTION

In our work, we've met hundreds of clients who carry the burden of self-hatred. One of them was Robert, a 52-year-old finance professional. On paper, he had achieved a great deal: a solid career, a family, a stable life. But emotionally, he was worn down. Years of unfulfilling relationships and heartbreaks had left him questioning his self-worth. Over time, that uncertainty hardened into something more painful: a deep-seated belief that he was unlovable.

Early wounds
Robert's struggle began long before adulthood. As a teenager, he was bullied for his weight and quiet nature, subtle cruelties that left deep marks. These early experiences planted the seeds of self-doubt, and as the years passed, those doubts grew. No matter how successful he became professionally, Robert couldn't silence the inner voice that told him he wasn't good enough, especially when it came to romantic relationships.

A world without truth
Without the safety or support to come out when he was young, Robert built a life within the heterosexual world. He married, had children, and tried to make it work. For many years, he suppressed his sexuality. But eventually, the weight of that denial became too heavy. The strength to come out to his family and friends was a huge personal milestone, yet it didn't bring the connection he'd hoped for. He struggled to meet other gay

men and was lost in a world that seemed to prize surface-level attraction over genuine connection.

Comparison as a form of self-hate

With the encouragement of friends, Robert began trying to meet people online. But the experience left him more isolated than ever. Going through dating apps, which often prioritise looks, only worsened his self-doubt. Every time he didn't get a match, the old voice of self-doubt would return: *If only I were more attractive, people would want to date me.*

Even when he did match with someone and made it to a date, his confidence would unravel. He second-guessed his every word, worried about how he was coming across, and often appeared nervous and unsure.

The competitive world of dating apps seemed like a popularity contest he could never win. He'd compare himself to the polished profiles he saw: *They're better looking, more interesting, more successful, why would anyone choose me?* That constant internal comparison wore him down until he questioned whether he should be dating at all.

'I blew it, again'

One experience in particular hit hard. Robert had been chatting with someone he really liked. After a few weeks of promising conversation, they arranged to meet. Robert spent hours preparing, but on the date, he couldn't relax. His mind was racing: *Why did I say that? That was so stupid. I bet he's not interested anymore. I'm such a failure at this.*

When he didn't hear back, it confirmed his worst fears. To Robert, it wasn't just a disappointing date; it was proof that he was broken.

After that, he stopped dating altogether and began to retreat emotionally. His self-worth was at an all-time low, and he didn't know how to climb out of the spiral.

A different kind of help

This was the point where Robert reached out to us. He was hesitant. He'd tried therapy. He'd read the self-help books. Still, the belief that he was unlovable persisted. But what he hadn't yet tried was working with people who truly understood the specific challenges of gay men looking for love, not on a screen, but in real life. Andrea and I worked closely with him. We did not begin with dating tactics. We began by rebuilding his relationship with himself.

Challenge the inner critic

One of our first steps was to help Robert challenge his negative self-talk. Those cruel, automatic thoughts had gone unexamined for too long. We introduced tools such as journaling and affirmations, simple but powerful ways for him to reconnect with his strengths. Bit by bit, Robert began to recognise the qualities that made him unique and worthy: his warmth, his loyalty, his curiosity.

Building skills and confidence

We also helped Robert refine his social skills, not to 'perform' better on dates, but to be himself. We worked on conversation techniques, body language, and ways to manage anxiety. We reminded him that dating isn't about impressing people; it's about making a genuine connection. Perfection isn't the goal. Presence is.

Robert also joined one of our group workshops. There, he met other gay men who shared similar stories; men who, like him, had faced rejection, carried old wounds, and still wanted to believe in love. That community was transformative. For the first time, Robert didn't pretend. He was seen.

A shift in perspective

Over time, Robert's outlook on dating changed. He began to approach each new connection with openness and curiosity, rather than fear. Rejection still stung, but it no longer defined him. He began to see it as a normal part of dating, not a personal verdict.

Then Robert met someone through our service. What made this different was not that he finally 'won' at dating; it was that he showed up as himself. He didn't hide, perform, or panic. He connected.

The ensuing relationship was based on mutual respect, kindness and authenticity. It wasn't a fairy tale; it was real. And that was enough.

MY PATH FROM SELF-HATRED TO SELF-LOVE

Discovering my truth and living as an openly gay man, and now supporting the gay community to find love, is the most humbling thing I have ever done, apart from creating my relationship with Andrea and finding the strength to sustain it in today's world.

I grew up in the vibrant, often turbulent 1970s and 1980s, which shaped me in ways I only began to understand in the 1990s. I navigated the tricky waters of self-discovery against a backdrop of societal pressure and private struggle. As you know from earlier in this book, I was born into a Croatian Catholic family. My upbringing was steeped in tradition and expectation. I carried the weight of these norms like a cloak, hiding the truth of who I was.

From a young age, I knew I was unlike others. The norms of the time painted a rigid picture of masculinity with no room for difference. This was an era of rebellion for many, but for me, it was a time of deep inner conflict. I feared abandonment. I feared being left because of who I was. This haunted me. The thought of revealing my true self wasn't simply intimidating. It seemed impossible.

That fear fed an overwhelming sense of self-hatred. It was a hard time to be gay. Judgement was everywhere, and it sank in deep. The Catholic teachings I had grown up with clashed with my inner convictions, setting off a long cycle of guilt and shame that seemed like it would never end.

As I grew older, the pressure to break free grew too. Courage didn't arrive in a flash. It came in pieces. One of those turning points was my decision to come out, a process that began far from home in London. The distance gave me breathing space, to begin unwinding the knots I'd carried for years.

Crafting letters and making phone calls to my family from London was both emotional and freeing. It was an act of defiance against the self-hatred I had lived with for so long. I was scared of rejection, but I was more scared of living a lie. Coming out wasn't just about being open. It was about shedding years of shame and stepping into something honest.

The struggle didn't vanish overnight. The old norms still held power, and the shame took time to loosen its grip. But every step forward, every act of self-respect, helped piece me back together. I started to see myself with kindness. I started to believe I was worth loving.

Those years were tough. But they were also the bridge from self-hatred to self-acceptance. I feared, but I also found courage. I experienced shame, but I discovered pride. And in the end, I found peace. The work of self-discovery goes on, but the ground I built during those years gave me something solid. I no longer apologise for who I am.

RISKS OF LEAVING SELF-HATRED UNADDRESSED

Untreated shame and self-hatred have terrible consequences. As gay men, we can't afford to ignore self-hatred. We must treat the pain inflicted on us by social stigma and condemnation. In our work, Andrea and I have seen the results of leaving self-hatred untreated:

Depression
The sense of not being good enough or lovable leads to depression. The pressure to fit into a hetero-normative world makes this worse, creating isolation and despair.

Anxiety
Concealing your identity and living in fear of rejection creates a constant tension. This stress affects every part of one's life and makes it hard to function day to day.

Substance abuse
To numb the pain of shame and mental distress, some gay men turn to alcohol or drugs. It offers short-term relief, but it creates more damage and spirals out of control.

Self-harm and suicidal thoughts
In some cases, the weight of self-hatred becomes too much. Rates of suicide and self-harm are higher among LGBTQIA+ people than among our heterosexual peers. If this is something you're facing, please talk to medical professionals or call Lifeline Australia on 13 11 14.

DEDICATE YOURSELF TO HEALING

Healing from self-hatred takes time, commitment and community support. You don't have to do this alone.

Mental health support
Choose professionals who understand your lived experience. LGBTQIA+-affirming therapists, counsellors and support groups will help you unpack the roots of self-hatred and assist you as you start to build a stronger, kinder relationship with yourself.

Positive representation
Look for role models and stories that reflect your worth. Seeing confident, joyful LGBTQIA+ people in the media will shift how you see yourself. Representation matters; it reminds you that love, success and belonging are possible.

Educational initiatives
When schools and communities include LGBTQIA+ education, it changes social attitudes. Let's help all children learn about Queer history, identity and rights to reduce stigma and build understanding. The earlier this happens, the better.

Supportive environments
Be with safe people and go to safe places. Acceptance, whether at home, at work or socialising, lessens self-doubt. When others treat you with respect, it becomes easier to offer the same to yourself.

LOVE EACH OTHER AS A COMMUNITY

For me, self-hatred is a powerful subject. It carries deep weight on its own, and when society reinforces it, the impact on our mental health and relationships can be devastating. I see this in my work, which is why I care deeply about what I do.

To shift this, we need more than personal effort; we need support systems, visible role models and cultural change. Together, these shape spaces where people can grow and build strong, healthy relationships.

As gay men, we must face homophobia not just from outside our community, but also from within. Let's stand together, not pull each other down. While external discrimination creates real barriers, our own divisions make those barriers grow even taller.

Like every community, ours is rich with diversity. That diversity is a strength. But it also becomes a source of separation. When we sort ourselves by body type, age, race or interests, we risk building walls where we should be building bridges, and weaken the unity we need to face homophobia with strength.

Here are some ways we see division:

Racial divisions

Racial and ethnic minority gay men face discrimination not just from the world at large, but from within the LGBTQIA+ community. This exclusion leaves them isolated and unsupported, cut off from a sense of belonging.

Body image and ageism

When we idealise certain body types or prize youth over experience, we send a message that only some people matter. Those who don't match that image find themselves pushed aside, unseen and undervalued.

Social cliques
When we form cliques around lifestyle or interests, we close ourselves off without meaning to. If someone doesn't fit, they feel judged or excluded. That sense of not belonging deepens self-doubt and keeps us from the connection we crave.

LET'S DO THIS
If we want to reduce homophobia and strengthen our community, we need to close the gaps between us. That means creating strong, inclusive support systems that welcome everyone. Here are few ways we can start:

- Make inclusivity part of everything we do, from our events and conversations to the spaces we create.
- Host gatherings that welcome people of all backgrounds, body types and ages, not only the ones who look or act like us.
- Focus on building spaces where people are valued and safe, that's how we break down barriers.

Let's stop judging and start connecting. When we honour the experiences of people who don't look or live like us, we build something stronger. By embracing difference, we celebrate who we are, and we grow more resilient.

We lead best when we lead by example. Every one of us has the power to change things. As individuals, we are kind, thoughtful, curious, generous and genuine. But as a community, we don't reflect those values to each other.

We can change that. Let's widen our social circles and include people with different life experiences. Small acts of welcome, such as inviting someone to join in, listening with care, speaking up when something's not right, shift the whole dynamic. We support each other when we speak out against exclusion, and build safer, more connected spaces.

The world seems fragile right now. We are unsure where society is heading. But you can offer kindness. You can show love.

Yes, our community faces serious challenges from outside. But if we don't heal the divisions inside, we weaken ourselves. Let's build something better together, something inclusive, open and strong. Let's stop being our own worst critics. Let's become each other's allies.

CONCLUSION

In the journey of overcoming self-hatred, empathy, help and love play a vital role in transforming our inner world. Self-hatred stems from deep wounds and a place of feeling unworthy or unloved. It is an overwhelming burden to carry. But, as I've learned through my own struggles, the path to healing is paved with understanding and compassion, both for ourselves and those who care for us.

Compassion allows you to acknowledge the struggles you have faced without judgement. This understanding, when met with genuine care from those around us, becomes a powerful force for change. Care isn't just about offering solutions.

It's about being there, standing by someone's side and offering a hand to hold during the darkest moments.

But above all, it's love that heals. Love, unconditional, unwavering and steadfast has the power to dissolve even the deepest self-loathing. When we are loved, not despite our flaws, but because of them, we see ourselves as worthy of that love. Through the love of others, we learn to love ourselves piece by piece until the walls we've built around our hearts crumble.

The journey from self-hatred to self-acceptance is not one we take alone. We must find the courage to reach out, welcome others to walk with us and embrace the kindness they offer. It's a journey that demands patience for ourselves and those who join us. But in the end, it is this combination of empathy, understanding and love that lights the way, helping us to see ourselves not as broken but as whole and deserving of the good that life offers.

In these moments of connection and understanding, we find the heart of what it means to heal, to let go of the shame, to forgive ourselves and to move forward with a renewed sense of purpose and hope.

CHAPTER SIX

Dating with HIV

This chapter is for those of us living with HIV, and for those who are not. Today, understanding the risks makes a huge difference to your chances of finding lasting love. This is a story about how hard it can be to disclose your HIV status. In many ways, it's also a cautionary tale about how not to do so. I am proud to share how I disclosed my HIV status to Andrea, a story I am now open about, but which caused a lot of angst along the way.

A TEST OF LOVE

When Andrea and I first got together, I made a decision that shaped the start of our relationship in ways neither of us could have imagined. I chose not to disclose my HIV status to him. Of course, I always made sure Andrea was safe. His wellbeing was my top priority.

My HIV status, in medical terms, is 'undetectable'. The medication I take causes viral suppression, which reduces the virus to undetectable levels in my blood. Viral suppression is defined as having less than 200 copies of HIV per millilitre of blood. It keeps me healthy and prevents transmission.

Getting to and keeping an undetectable viral load is the best thing people with HIV can do to stay healthy. People with HIV who take their medicine as prescribed and keep an undetectable viral load will not transmit HIV to their partners. This is called 'undetectable = untransmittable' or U=U.

I did not doubt Andrea's love. I believed in the strength of our bond, and I hoped it was stronger than the stigma surrounding the virus. But I knew Andrea didn't have much education on the subject and that gap in knowledge weighed heavily on me. I was afraid. Even though, deep down, I wanted to believe he would be okay with my HIV status if he truly understood that he was not at risk of infection, I feared rejection.

The decision not to tell Andrea about my HIV was one of the hardest in my life. Until then, I was always open and direct with everyone. I accepted my status long ago and learned to live with it positively, and always openly shared it with close friends and partners in previous relationships. I look after myself meticulously and have check-ups every two months to ensure I stay undetectable.

When I was diagnosed, it was a turning point. I became determined to live a healthier life. I embraced yoga and meditation practices and cultivated a deep respect for the preciousness of life. I found myself saying that, in some strange ways, contracting HIV was a good thing for me. It sharpened my resolve, made me more successful in my private life, and gave me a clarity of purpose that I hadn't known before. I learned to respect life and its fragility. HIV changed my life in profound ways and, in many respects, it changed me for the better.

But even with this positive outlook, I couldn't escape the fear that came with my status, a fear that made me keep it a secret from Andrea. Every day I held onto the secret, I was risking everything. The secret was a crushing weight. I lived in constant fear of losing him if he ever found out the truth from someone else.

In some ways I felt that the secret protected him. In our early years in Australia, he knew few people who could support him. But at the same time, it was killing me that I couldn't be open and honest with the man I loved more than anything.

I tried to bring it up several times. I looked for the right moment to tell him. But it never came. The words would get stuck in my throat, or the conversation would veer off in another direction. I was left frustrated and defeated.

I wrote many letters to Andrea with the truth, letters that I did not send. Here is one that I found while researching this book. In it, you can hear my fear and love, and my effort to be brave.

Dearest Andrea,

There is no hour that goes by that I don't think about how you are doing or about the words you have written to me. Your thoughts and ideas have sparked so many feelings in me, not least of which is love. Through our letters, you have awakened a depth of emotion in me that I haven't felt in a long time, especially in matters of romance and connection.

In our journey together, I have come to understand the power of being truly seen by someone else. It is a beautiful and rare thing to feel that someone understands you as deeply as you understand yourself. This mutual understanding makes falling in love so effortless, and perhaps this is what has been happening between us.

Yet, as we grow closer, I find myself grappling with a truth that I need to share with you. It's something that weighs on my heart because I love you and fear losing you. But our love deserves honesty, and you deserve to know all of me.

I am HIV-positive and undetectable. This means that while I carry the virus, the treatment I undergo keeps it at levels so low that it cannot be transmitted to others. It's a medical breakthrough that has transformed lives, including mine. But I know that this truth might come as a shock, and it terrifies me to think of what it might mean for us.

I am afraid that this conversation might lead to heartbreak. The stigma and fear around HIV are pervasive and I know that many would say no to a relationship with someone who is positive. I believe in our love and the understanding we've built together, yet I have so much fear in myself.

Being open with you about this is not just about my health status; it's about the future I see for us, a future where we continue to share, grow, and love each other without secrets or fears. I have always wanted to create a safe space for people living with HIV, where they can love and be loved without the shadow of their condition. I dream of that same safe space for us.

When I see you, I see someone who sees me for who I truly am, and that is a powerful and wonderful thing.

It gives me hope that you can accept this part of me too. I want to reach out to you, both physically and emotionally, and let you know that my feelings for you are real and deep.

Understanding and loving each other means being open to all aspects of our lives. It's about creating a union where both of us feel safe, respected, and cherished. My heart tells me that you are someone who can see beyond the surface, someone who values the person I am and not just the circumstances of my life.

I believe in the love we share, and I hope this truth strengthens our bond rather than weakening it. Please know that I am here to talk, to answer any questions you have, and to continue building a future together, one filled with love, compassion, and mutual respect.

With all my love,
Vinko

I could not send this or any of the other letters I wrote to him. Andrea never asked about my HIV status, I never raised it, and our friends all assumed he knew, so it never came up. Looking back, I thought that he would not understand it; perhaps he didn't know much about the reality of being HIV because he didn't have to. Revealing your HIV status is a bitch.

But the longer I kept the secret, the heavier it became and the more it eroded my peace of mind.

Finally, after five years – yes, five years – I reached a point where I knew I couldn't keep it hidden any longer. Andrea's knowledge of HIV had grown, and I felt he now had enough support and knowledge to handle the truth.

COURAGE COMES

One morning, before I went to work, I left my HIV prevention pills on the bathroom sink deliberately, so Andrea would see them when he woke up. It wasn't the most direct approach, but I felt it was the best way to give him time to process the news without the pressure of an immediate conversation.

That day was the toughest of my life. My heart pounded as I left the house, unsure of what I would come home to. I believed in us. I believed in our love. I knew that Andrea would understand my desire to protect him. Still, I couldn't shake the fear that my dishonesty could unravel what we had built together.

When I returned home that evening, Andrea was waiting for me. There was a moment of silence before he spoke and, in that moment, I saw the love in his eyes. It was mixed with confusion and hurt, but also with understanding. We talked for hours that night, about my status, why I had kept it from him and how much I loved him. It was one of the most intense conversations between us. But it liberated me. The truth was out and, for the first time in five years, I could breathe again. Andrea showed the kind of grace that only comes from real love.

He didn't raise his voice; he didn't turn away. Instead, he quietly took it upon himself to get tested, to face whatever fears might have crept in, not for drama or blame, but to protect his own peace and dignity. From the very start, he was respectful and kind, though perhaps, back when he knew so little about HIV beyond fear and stigma, he might not have had the courage to keep walking forward with me. Not because he didn't love me, but because he wouldn't have known better. In a way, though the path was imperfect, he was grateful for how it unfolded, grateful that love had the time to grow stronger than fear, that trust had time to take root.

That's the kind of man Andrea is. His love is not loud, it's not performative; it's steadfast. It's a love that holds you when you think you might fall and stays standing even when the truth shakes the ground beneath you. And it is that love that taught me that the right person will love you despite your story

Today, I still believe I made the right decision, even though it was an agonising one. I'm not entirely sure there would still be an 'us' if we hadn't spent those years building a world together, getting to know each other on the deepest level and creating a love strong enough to support this truth. I wish it could have been different. Living with that secret for five years was incredibly painful and it's not something I would ever recommend.

DO WHAT I SAY, NOT WHAT I DO

If you are in a similar situation, I urge you to discuss your status openly with your partner from the beginning. Make sure the other person is safe and let them make the decision themselves. I was lucky. Andrea's love and support did not waver. When the truth finally came out, it transformed our relationship. There were no more secrets and not having to hide anymore changed my life.

No longer hiding my status brought me a newfound freedom, and it altered how I approached everything: life, love, money and my day-to-day existence. Living authentically without that burden made everything easier and more fulfilling. There's a certain kind of strength that only comes when you know you have nothing left to lose. For so long, carrying that secret had kept a quiet fear alive inside me, the fear of losing everything if the truth ever came out. It shaped the way I moved, the way I loved, the way I trusted. But once the weight of that fear was lifted, something in me shifted forever. I no longer lived half-held back by worry or shame. I became fiercer, stronger, clearer.

There was no stopping me anymore, no second-guessing my worth, no shrinking to fit into anyone else's comfort. I finally knew that the life I was building was rooted in truth, and from that place, real power began to grow. Our relationship, our business and our friendships just became stronger and stronger.

A SAFE SPACE FOR HIV-POSITIVE DATING

In the past 15 years, as co-founder of BBI, I have had the privilege of being part of a profound transformation in attitudes among gay men towards long-term relationships. I am deeply committed to creating a safe and inclusive environment for all. Witnessing more men being open to dating men who are HIV-positive has been one of the most heartening changes in my career.

When we began BBI, the landscape was starkly different. Approximately 80 per cent of our clients declined to meet someone who was HIV-positive, even if that person had an undetectable viral load. This widespread rejection stemmed from fear and misinformation. It was a heartbreaking reality for many of our clients who were living with the virus. They faced the challenge of managing their health, the daunting task of disclosing their status to potential partners and the emotional toll of constant rejection.

From the beginning, my mission was to create a safe space where everyone, regardless of their HIV status, could find love and companionship without fear of judgement or rejection. I wanted to ensure that every person who came to us felt valued and respected and that their search for love would not be hindered by their health status.

Education is the key
In those early days, providing this kind of safety required significant effort and compassion. We had to work diligently to educate our clients about HIV, the advancements in treatment and the significance of being undetectable. We organised workshops and talked to medical experts to educate ourselves. We shared stories of successful loving relationships where one partner was HIV-positive. It was a gradual process, but every small step forward felt like a victory.

The turning point came as medical advancements continued to improve the lives of those living with HIV. The introduction of antiretroviral therapy (ART) and the widespread understanding of U=U played a crucial role in changing public perception. People began to realise that an undetectable viral load meant that HIV could not be transmitted to partners, fundamentally altering the dynamics of dating and relationships.

Today, I am overjoyed to report that about 90 per cent of our clients are open to meeting and dating someone who is HIV-positive and undetectable, regardless of their own status. This remarkable shift in attitudes has been nothing short of revolutionary. It is a testament to the power of education, empathy and the resilience of our community.

A BRIEF HISTORY OF HIV/AIDS

In the early 1980s, the emergence of HIV/AIDS marked the beginning of a global health crisis. Initially labelled by some in the media the 'gay plague', the disease was shrouded in fear and misinformation. At first, we had no effective treatments. The virus spread rapidly and killed so many young gay men, and others. It was heartbreaking. The social stigma surrounding HIV/AIDS made the suffering so much worse. Many died alone, unsupported and cast out by family and even friends.

The identification of HIV as the causative agent of AIDS in 1983 was a turning point, enabling scientists to develop targeted interventions. The arrival of ART in the mid-1990s transformed HIV from a fatal disease into a manageable chronic condition. The medications work by suppressing the viral load in a person's body, preventing the progression to AIDS and reducing the risk of transmission.

ART was a game-changer for people dating with HIV. They could now lead long, healthy lives with proper treatment and care. Additionally, the concept of U=U shows that individuals with an undetectable viral load cannot transmit the virus to others. This breakthrough has improved the lives of those living with HIV and significantly reduced the shame associated with the virus.

Advances in medical research, treatment and societal attitudes have created a more supportive environment for those affected by the virus. However, challenges remain. The experience of living with HIV is affected by several factors, including access to healthcare, social support and individual circumstances.

ACCESS IS NOT EQUAL

Access to healthcare and ART allows us to manage HIV. In many parts of the world, such as here in Australia, ART is readily available, and regular monitoring ensures that we maintain an undetectable viral load. However, disparities in healthcare access persist, particularly in countries with low- and middle-income economies. There are ongoing initiatives aimed at increasing ART availability and improving healthcare infrastructure by so many organisations, such as UNAIDS, the Global Fund to Fight AIDS, Tuberculosis and Malaria, PEPFAR (United States President's Emergency Plan For AIDS Relief), and the World Health Organization (WHO). These organisations fund programs, negotiate lower medication costs, and support healthcare infrastructure improvements worldwide. Some specific initiatives include providing free or low-cost

ART, supporting community health workers, expanding HIV testing and counselling services, and working towards the goal of ending the AIDS epidemic as a public health threat by 2030. Today, work still needs to be done globally to close the gap and make effective HIV care accessible to all.

Discrimination continues to affect people living with HIV. Misconceptions about the virus, fear of transmission and moral judgements mean we sometimes feel socially excluded and have mental health challenges. Andrea and I have done a lot of education and awareness raising in our business. Government campaigns also play a role in fostering a more inclusive and understanding society.

RESEARCH CONTINUES

Preventing HIV transmission is the best strategy for eliminating the virus. Pre-exposure prophylaxis (PrEP) is a highly effective preventive measure for individuals at high risk of contracting HIV. PrEP involves taking a daily medication that significantly reduces the risk of HIV infection. Widespread awareness and access to PrEP can further reduce new HIV transmissions.

Ongoing research continues to explore new treatment options, vaccines and potential cures for HIV. Long-acting injectable ART, for example, offers a promising alternative to daily medication regimens. Advances in gene therapy and immunotherapy also hold potential for future breakthroughs in HIV treatment and prevention.

While remarkable progress has been made, our community must continue its efforts to ensure equitable access to healthcare worldwide, combat discrimination and help those living with HIV. We must keep the need for international collaboration, community engagement and sustained investment in the minds of health decision makers.

HARDER TO BE HAPPY

Despite all the advances, living with HIV has psychological impacts, such as anxiety, depression and isolation. Our clients living with HIV often talk about feeling despondent, depressed and, at times, not accepted by their colleagues, their families or themselves. The social structures that support heterosexuality as the norm are internalised by everyone, making society's judgements influence their own self-judgement.

German philosopher Georg Wilhelm Friedrich Hegel (1770–1831) wrote that those with less power often see themselves through the eyes of the powerful. That's what stigma does; it teaches us to judge ourselves.

Negative self-judgement often lies at the heart of gay life and relationships. Learning to love in a culture with few representations of men loving men is difficult. The pursuit of pleasure can be a rebellion against, or an antidote to, the depression and melancholy that threaten to overwhelm us. It is also a form of defiance against normative heterosexual ideals. However, this search for pleasure often does not satisfy our deeper need for acceptance, belonging, love, safety and affirmation. If the desire for a committed relationship stems from a need to compensate for self-rejection, it can be difficult to love your partner or accept his love genuinely. Finding a partner who desires commitment can be the beginning of a long struggle against self-hatred and towards self-acceptance, as we discussed in Chapter 5.

Our book is called *All In* because it is about commitment, regardless of the circumstances or hurdles life presents. We all want different things out of life and may yearn to settle down. This concept can be challenging within gay culture. Is the pursuit of orgiastic pleasure also about avoiding self-doubt and judgement? Has living with HIV made this more difficult? Is the thrill of the chase absent in a steady relationship, leading to fears that sexual desire will die?

The transition away from seeking random sexual gratification is fraught with difficulty. Love has many modes of expression, not just sexuality. If your sexuality is linked with HIV and self-rejection, this transition can be particularly challenging.

We all desire companionship. But those living with HIV might also struggle with self-acceptance, making the prospect of finding or engaging in a relationship daunting.

Support systems such as counselling, support groups and community organisations provide emotional and psychological assistance. These resources can help you cope with your diagnosis and build resilience.

HAPPY ALONE, HAPPY TOGETHER

I am HIV-positive. I still struggle to accept that I am no different to other people if I look after myself and respect and accept myself. I have always believed that before you can build something lasting with another person, you must find peace in being alone. You must be your own safe place first. Needing validation from your lover often leads to relationships that feel heavy, fragile, or even destructive.

But if I am honest with myself, I can see that, for a long time, I was seeking a kind of validation from others, permission to feel good enough, whole enough, lovable enough. Deep down, there were times I didn't fully feel that way about myself.

This is part of the reason why, before Andrea, I was always very open about my HIV status with everyone I met. It wasn't just honesty; it was a way of trying to control the fear of rejection, a way to say, 'Here I am, take it or leave it', before they had a chance to find something 'wrong' with me. It was a shield, but also a silent plea for acceptance.

'Having someone to come home to' means different things to different people. For some, it's about companionship, sharing meals, or having someone to listen to you and talk with at the end of a hard day. For me, it has always been deeper than that: I wanted someone I didn't have to explain myself to. Someone who would see it all – the fears, the history, the tenderness – and still stay.

There is a broad range of what my clients have in mind when they long for someone to come home to.

'COMING OUT' ABOUT HIV

Choosing to be open about your HIV status can lift the heavy burden of secrecy and shame. It is an act of courage, a way of reclaiming your story and stepping into your own light. Yet even after coming out, it's natural to sometimes feel the urge to hide parts of ourselves behind different masks. We may still wrestle with moments of self-rejection, shaped by years of societal judgement and expectations. It's not a failure; it's a reflection of the world we've had to survive in. Learning to recognise these layers with compassion, and to challenge the norms that made us feel unworthy in the first place, is part of the journey towards true belonging. The life and love we deserve must first be recognised and embraced within us, and from there, everything else can begin.

There comes a moment, after diagnosis, after fear, after shame, when the real work of healing begins. It doesn't start with medicine. It doesn't even start with others. It starts deep inside, with the willingness to see ourselves differently.

THREE ONGOING STEPS

The process of truly living with HIV, of truly living as a proud gay man in a world that often misunderstands us, involves three ongoing, imperfect, beautiful steps. They are not linear. We circle through them again and again, each time coming home to ourselves a little more whole, a little freer.

Step one: Understand the full picture of health
Caring for our bodies is an act of love, not fear. Of course, HIV isn't the only health issue we face as gay men. Understanding the full landscape of sexual health is empowering; it's about keeping ourselves and our partners safe without shame or secrecy.

We face risks such as human papillomavirus (HPV), herpes, syphilis, hepatitis, trichomoniasis, gonorrhoea and chlamydia. But knowledge is not a burden; it is a tool for freedom. Regular checkups, vaccines and treatments are acts of care, of valuing our lives enough to protect them. Our health challenges do not define us; our courage in facing them does.

Step two: Recognise and challenge the norms
Beneath the surface of our lives run quiet stories, the societal norms that taught us to question our worth, to hide our vulnerabilities, to see ourselves through a lens of shame. Recognising these inherited beliefs is not easy. Changing them is harder still.

But it begins with awareness. Practices like yoga and meditation became, for me, small rebellions, spaces where I affirmed my existence, my dignity, my right to love and be loved without apology.

We must celebrate not fitting in. We must see the beauty in nonconformity. And we must remember: the burden of creative evolution should not fall only on those who already carry so much. We all have a role to play in building a world that embraces difference rather than fears it.

Step three: Learn to love oneself, and another
Perhaps the most radical act of all is simply to love ourselves, even when the world has given us a thousand reasons not to. This isn't a fairy tale where self-love magically leads to a 'happily ever after'. It is harder, messier and more beautiful than that.

Living with HIV often felt, at first, like wearing a mask, a mask that indicated to others: *You are damaged.* But over time, I understood that the damage was never mine. The shame was never mine. The fear was never mine.

Since my diagnosis, I have learned – and I am still learning – to love myself as a man living with HIV, a man who deserves tenderness, stability, commitment, adventure, tears, joy, and a home filled with real, unconditional love.

I have learned that my grief does not cancel my hope. That my sadness does not cancel my beauty. That my diagnosis does not cancel my humanity.

This is not a story about surviving; it's a story about living fully, deeply, fiercely. And it begins with one quiet, undeniable truth: We are already enough.

CONCLUSION

The story of revealing HIV status is not just about statistics. It's about real people finding love and acceptance. Andrea and I want to create a world where everyone can build meaningful connections, without misconceptions about HIV hanging over them. We also honour the humanity and dignity of each person who walks through our doors.

The story of HIV underscores the power of science, advocacy and human compassion. Living with HIV now means having the opportunity to thrive, love and contribute to society, free from the constraints of a once-deadly disease. The future holds the promise of further progress, with the goal of ending the HIV epidemic and ensuring that, regardless of their HIV status, everyone can live a healthy and fulfilling life.

I know how living with HIV comes with its own unique pain, especially when having those difficult conversations with someone you love. No matter how many letters you write or how many times you rehearse the conversation, it requires time and courage to speak the words.

When I reflect on the past, I am filled with gratitude and pride. The journey has not been easy, but the progress we have made as a community is inspiring. We have shown that love transcends fear and ignorance, that compassion and understanding can overcome prejudice, and that everyone deserves a chance to find their perfect match.

As we look to the future, I remain committed to this mission. There is still work to be done, but I am confident we are moving in the right direction. Together we will continue to break down barriers, challenge misconceptions and create a world where love knows no bounds.

To all those who have been part of this journey, thank you. Your courage, openness and willingness to embrace change have made all the difference. Here's to many more years of love, acceptance and happiness for everyone in our community.

CHAPTER SEVEN

Jouissance: Pleasure beyond safety

When you meet a man who completely lights you up – someone who radiates beauty, charm, confidence and desire – you don't stay the same. Something shifts. You are drawn out of yourself. You're caught in that rush of energy where pleasure mixes with awe, and the ordinary suddenly feels extraordinary. The French psychoanalyst Jacques Lacan,[1] who reshaped modern understandings of desire and identity, had a word for that: *jouissance*.

The French word, *jouissance*, usually translates as 'enjoyment', 'bliss' or even 'orgasm'. But Lacan meant something deeper, stranger, more intense. He saw jouissance as pleasure that crosses a line; not soft or safe. It often involves discomfort, even pain. But in the intensity of jouissance, in the loss of control, you feel something powerful: 'desire breaking through the surface', by which he meant a moment when unconscious longing erupts into conscious experience, disrupting the roles you usually perform and revealing what you truly want.

---

[1] Lacan showed how we are formed not just by our feelings, but by language, symbols and how others see us. He was a practising psychoanalyst and a charismatic lecturer at the École Freudienne de Paris.

Lacan believed we are all shaped by a kind of longing. You are always reaching for something you don't fully understand, something just out of reach. Jouissance is what you feel in the pursuit of that unreachable desire. It's where pleasure meets risk, where the usual limits of self-control, identity, or social roles start to dissolve, and you lose yourself in the other.

Sometimes it's mutual. Sometimes it's not. But when two people feel mutual emotional or physical connection – when both feel seen, desired and accepted exactly as they are – jouissance can feel like a kind of truth. It's not that jouissance tells you the 'truth' in a factual sense, but that it taps into a deep, often hidden truth about what you long for, who you are, or what it feels like to be fully seen. A recognition. A deep 'Yes'. Your body knows before your mind does: in the touch, the taste, the breath between you.

I remember that moment with Andrea. We were both at turning points, the end of other relationships. Something between us felt immediate and clear. The spark wasn't just about attraction; it was about recognition. It felt like we could be fully ourselves. That, to me, is jouissance. Not just pleasure, not just excitement, but the sense that something real had shifted. That we had arrived in each other's lives at exactly the right moment.

Our first interaction was marked by playful banter. Andrea, with a cheeky grin, teased me at the beach about the way I splashed in the water like a carefree child. I responded with a light-hearted joke about seeing him dancing naked on a rock, without any music, like no-one was watching. Seeing him do this was one of the most beautiful visions of my life. I am sure you get my gist. Italian, tall, dark, handsome and, on top of it, naked! Andrea's eyes twinkled with mischief. It was in these moments that our bond began to form, rooted in a shared sense of joy and an appreciation for life's simple pleasures.

As the day progressed, we found ourselves drawn closer together, not just by the beauty surrounding us but by the palpable energy that crackled between us. We talked about our dreams, passions and visions for the future, as well as our existing lives and livelihoods. With each word, it became clear that our connection was more than a fleeting attraction, it was the beginning of something profound.

Our conversations were filled with hope and excitement. We realised that together we could build a life that was rich in love and shared dreams. The sense of freedom we felt in our location, which was Lokrum, an island in the Adriatic Sea, not far from the city of Dubrovnik, Croatia. This mirrored the freedom we found in each other's company. It was a freedom to be ourselves, to love openly and to achieve great things together. I knew instantly that with this person beside me, I could achieve anything in life.

Later, friends would recount how obvious the connection between us had been from the start. They spoke of the undeniable energy that surrounded us that day, a force so strong that it was clear to everyone else even before the two of us fully understood it. It was as if the universe had conspired to bring us together, aligning our paths in a moment of pure magic.

From the first cheeky remark and the first shared laugh to the moment our eyes locked in understanding, we knew there was something special between us. Our connection offered hope and the promise of a future where we could achieve anything together. It was the beginning of a beautiful journey, one that would see us embrace life's adventures side by side, fuelled by the energy and love that first brought us together on that unforgettable day.

THE COMPLEXITY OF JOUISSANCE

Let me tell you a story about one-sided jouissance. When I was quite lonely, living on my own, I used to go for a walk at the end of the day along the beach near my house in Sydney. One day, I was surprised to see an acquaintance I had met through a mutual friend. We walked along together and talked. In my loneliness, I enjoyed finding someone to talk to. Our conversation was interesting. Each day, to my surprise, he was there again. I thought it was pure coincidence. He was intensely interested in what I thought and felt, which is, of course, irresistibly flattering.

One day, without thinking about it too much, I invited him back to my place for something to eat. Over that meal, I could see that he was not at all my kind of person. I found his vulnerability unattractive. But at the time I felt like a beggar in love, and that I couldn't afford to be choosey. I didn't resist his presence in my life.

When I had to travel to Europe for six weeks to see family, I discovered a serious problem. Every day, I received several emails from him, berating me for abandoning him and telling me of his extreme vulnerability and an illness he believed was brought about because of my absence. He was fixated on me. As soon as I recognised this, I told him we had to end our relationship. He was sure I had led him on. He felt we had a commitment to each other. I told him that, whatever it was, it was over. But he could not let it go. When I got home, he began to stalk me; he was obsessed, unable to comprehend or accept that I did not reciprocate his feelings. This is an example of the dangers of assuming the other feels as you feel

Here's an example of a different kind of jouissance. I have a dear friend who lives with his partner and both of their extended families. This is not a conventional relationship. It is not a sexual relationship. But this brings them both jouissance. I have no doubt they are together for life. What they share is life-giving to both. They genuinely love each other and would not do anything to disrupt their relationship. They enjoy going to the theatre and travelling together, among many other activities. The pleasure and significance of such a commitment, meeting their need for safety and security, cannot be underestimated in making for a viable life. It's not what I would choose, but that doesn't make it an illegitimate choice for others

An initial lighting up or a surge of jouissance can be many things. It might be shared or not, and it may be able to be sustained or not. It might, initially, be a vital ingredient to the connection, but something else may replace it. Routines may take control and make life a set of predictable repetitions, draining jouissance. For some people, it is precisely those predictable repetitions they crave to make them feel safe.

A safe relationship can be full of mutual respect, gentleness and care, and for many, that is their paramount need. Conversely, it may be full of attempts to control and limit each other, which is toxic.

Jouissance is the ongoing *raison d'être* of my relationships, but it is not the only reason couples might have for staying together. Dating couples need to know what they are looking for. If it is commitment and a safe and predictable life, maybe they are not so bothered after a while if this is not accompanied by joyful sex.

THE CHALLENGE OF SUSTAINING JOUISSANCE

My friend's father told me, sadly, that he thought the only thing men need is sex. He felt depressed by his wife's lack of interest in sex with him. Meanwhile, my friend's mother had an incredibly joyful sexual relationship with her lover. It wasn't sex that she objected to, but sex in the way her husband practised it. I can see her point. Her husband was riddled with self-pity and hatred for women. He thought men were violent in their marriages because they were not satisfied in bed (so it was the woman's fault). His wife knew how he felt and what he thought, and she would not let him near her precious body or inner world.

In my experience, we can become someone unfamiliar and behave in ways we didn't know we were capable of in a relationship, both in good ways and bad ways.

When it is good, it is an intoxicating joy to become someone new. To be loved is more than being recognised for who you already are. It is to find yourself becoming someone you hadn't even known was possible, someone exciting in unforeseen ways. Someone you couldn't be on your own. The encounter with the other, at its best, is not a repetition of a pre-imagined scenario but a surprising happening.

Can we sustain that sense of surprise and amazement? It's hard. The demands of everyday life do not make room for days and nights of glorious love. The carnival of love needs a lot of space, time and energy. It demands that we close our attention to anything or anyone else for a while.

Can dating couples sustain the jouissance and still manage to responsibly do their jobs and attend to their families and other relationships? Can they resist turning each other into a predictable person who seems just the same as them, who reflects the rightness of their choices back to them, and who makes them safe in a mundane, repetitive way that snuffs out the energy and joy that brought them together? Is it possible to have it all: the joy, the safety and the predictability?

In thinking about gay dating, there is the initial dilemma of finding the other with whom that elevated and joyful becoming is possible. There is the giving of permission to allow oneself to enter completely into the joy of it. Then there is the challenge of figuring out what it will take from each partner to turn that initial madness into something that is deeply satisfying and sustaining.

JOUISSANCE THROUGH SEPARATION AND SELF-DISCOVERY

Recently, Andrea went overseas for two months, and we were apart, something that rarely happens in our relationship because we live and work together. We agreed to the separation to pursue goals in each of our businesses. But once I was on my own, I felt unsteady. I missed Andrea's presence, his guidance, and the comfort of knowing he was just a room away. I found myself needing to be part of his day, to hear every detail. That longing shook my confidence. Was I being ignored, or was I just feeling insecure?

I realised I needed to create a sense of safety for myself. I had to rediscover jouissance on my own. So I turned to things I loved, the activities that made me feel grounded and alive. I started painting again, something I have often done but I've never made the commitment to hold an exhibition. In those moments, I reclaimed my independence and nurtured my own joy.

When I needed Andrea's support, I reached out. He didn't always reach out in return, at least not as often. But this difference in approach taught me something important: we all communicate love in different ways. His quiet didn't mean he cared less. Understanding this helped me grow, not just in the relationship, but in myself. I began to trust our connection more deeply, even across distance.

Those two months turned out to be a powerful time of growth for us. I learned that tending to my needs isn't selfish; it's essential. I'm the one responsible for my emotional wellbeing. That insight let me return to our relationship stronger, more grounded.

I also learned more about Andrea, how he moves through the world when I'm not beside him. At first, when I rang him, I told him how vulnerable I felt. I missed him deeply and wished I were with him. But as I settled, something shifted. I felt proud of his wins, grateful for the joy he found with friends. I gave him space to thrive in his own way. And when we reconnected, it felt richer, like we were bringing the best of ourselves back to one another.

Yes, the separation was hard. But it was also a gift. It reminded me why time apart matters, if there's trust and care. We made space for conversation, shared our needs, and created a shared understanding of what would help us both feel secure.

That time apart taught me the value of independence within love. It reminded me that time together is vital, but so is solitude. That balance helps both partners grow, so they can return to the relationship with energy, clarity and purpose. Those two months were a test of, and a testament to, the strength of our bond.

JOUISSANCE AND LOVE: A SUCCESS STORY

I want to share a Beau Brummell Introductions success story that relates to jouissance. It involves two men, who I will call Edward and Jonathan. It was a pure joy to work with them. Both live in the fast lane, against the backdrop of the iconic skyline and sparkling harbour of Sydney, Australia. Both men, distinguished by their successes and striking good looks, reached great heights in their careers. Yet, despite their accomplishments, they felt a void that could only be filled by a meaningful, loving relationship.

Without ever knowing each other, Edward and Jonathan were both driven by a deep passion and an unwavering commitment to finding a partner who understood them completely. Each spoke about this openly with full hearts in my get-to-know-you meetings. Each expressed their readiness to put all their energies into finding a relationship. They had spent years cultivating a profound understanding of themselves and what they desired in a partner. Their hearts were open, and their intentions were clear: they wanted to share their lives equally, giving and receiving love in a balanced, supportive partnership.

Their journey brought them to BBI at around the same time. When we met each man, we understood that each sought more than a match, they both sought someone who could appreciate the unique individuals they were. We were inspired by each man's genuine desire to find love and their readiness to invest in a relationship built on mutual respect and understanding. Putting them together seemed almost inevitable, but we never take a match for granted. We thought about it carefully and then introduced them to each other.

As the reports came through from both sides after the first date, Edward and Jonathan's connection was nothing short of magical. Their initial encounter was filled with laughter and a sense of ease that can only come from meeting someone who truly gets you. They bonded over shared passions, similar life goals and the excitement of exploring a future together. Their connection was immediate and deep, sparking a journey of discovery and love. Both accepted each other's pasts and challenges openly and were willing to build a life together, supporting one another. They understood from the word go that not all would be perfect in life, but together they were strong enough to achieve anything.

Our clients are not considered matched until their first anniversary together. We stay in touch and coach them through some of the more difficult initial stages. As Edward and Jonathan spent more time together, it became evident that they were perfectly suited for one another. They supported each other unconditionally, celebrated each other's successes and provided comfort during challenging times. Their relationship was a beautiful dance of give and take, where both men felt valued and understood.

Throughout their relationship, Edward and Jonathan continue to grow individually and as a couple. They inspire each other to be the best versions of themselves, pushing each other towards new heights. Their love story is a testament to the power of finding a partner who complements you in every way, someone who sees your worth and cherishes you for who you are.

At BBI, we take immense pride in the role we played in the love story between Edward and Jonathan. Their joy and commitment brought them together, and it was an honour to guide them on their path together. Our mission is to help clients find jouissance. For Edward and Jonathan, their journey was not just about finding love; it was about building a life together, filled with shared dreams and unwavering support.

Their story is a shining example of what two people can achieve when, full of passion and love, they come together with a shared goal. It reminds us that true love is possible with a little help. Their flourishing relationship is a beacon of hope and inspiration for all those still searching for their perfect match.

CONCLUSION

This chapter has explored jouissance not just as a rush of desire, but as a powerful moment of transformation. We've seen how jouissance can light up a connection, bring new energy into a relationship, and reveal parts of ourselves we hadn't yet met. But it can also unsettle or even destroy when it's not mutual, or when it's mistaken for something it's not.

We've looked at the difference between fleeting passion and sustainable joy. We've seen that one person's version of jouissance might be found in wild romance, while another's in companionship, consistency, or the quiet joy of daily rituals.

We've also examined the tension between freedom and safety, between becoming someone new in love and remaining grounded in who you are. And we've asked the hard question: Can we sustain the spark, or does it always burn out?

For jouissance to be joyful, it must be mutual. Don't assume that the spark you feel is also felt by the other person. It might be the beginning of something, or a beautiful moment that's not meant to last. When we confuse desire for destiny, we can find ourselves in the wrong story.

Start asking yourself what kind of relationship you really want. Do you crave excitement or safety? Do you want to be surprised or soothed? Do you long to be recognised, or to become someone new through love?

You don't have to know the answer straight away. But asking the question is where clarity begins.

And if jouissance opens the door, self-acceptance is what lets you walk through it with grace. In the next chapter, we'll explore what it really means to accept yourself, not just your sexuality, but your body, your needs, and your right to love and be loved exactly as you are.

CHAPTER EIGHT

Figuring it all out

Understanding and accepting your identity as a gay man is a deeply personal journey. It's not a single turning point, but a gradual process: sometimes uplifting, sometimes bruising. For many of us, the road includes familiar waypoints: the childhood realisation that we are 'different'; the shame of hiding; the first moment of desire that both thrills and terrifies; the courage to confide in someone we trust; the sting of rejection; and, eventually, the growing pride in living openly. This is not a neat sequence. You might navigate some or all of these paths, and experience moments of both clarity and confusion, as you take on the complex task of sharing your true self with the world.

In this chapter, I will share my struggle for acceptance, my story of self-discovery, and moments of clarity that brought me closer to my true self.

Is it possible to live a good life without going so deeply into self-acceptance? That's a fair question. For some, the idea of coming out at all is simply too painful, too entangled with family, faith, safety or survival. Others come out but never want to dwell too long in the past. They don't see the value in unpicking every memory. Detachment isn't always avoidance. It might be a boundary that makes sense to you. The cost of honesty can feel high, especially if past attempts were met with rejection or danger.

But if you've ever felt you were succeeding on the outside but shrinking on the inside, then self-acceptance might be what you're missing. It isn't just an emotional depth. It's existential. Abandon ourselves too often and we lose the thread of who we are. We go numb.

Self-acceptance doesn't mean settling. It doesn't mean saying, 'This is who I am, take it or leave it,' and never growing again. It's the opposite. It's the foundation that allows real growth to happen. Not from pressure or shame, but from care and self-trust.

This chapter is about the long, uneven road to self-acceptance. It's not a formula or a motivational tale. It's an honest look at the doubts, desires, mistakes and moments of clarity that shaped me. I am not trying to speak for everyone; I simply say that what we go through matters. The past shapes us. Sometimes it strengthens us. Sometimes it scars us. But if we're lucky, or stubborn enough, it can also become something we choose to understand rather than erase.

INNOCENCE AND LONGING

To achieve self-acceptance, we must return to the early years, before we had the words for difference, but when we were already absorbing messages about who we were allowed to be. The early years aren't just about family photos and vague memories. They're when we learn whether the world is safe or dangerous, whether love is earned or given freely. I think about a little kid I know who nearly died. I wonder what impact that early experience might have on his sense of safety in the world. Or of friends going through separation, and how their children might carry that emotional tension long after the dust settles. These early patterns shape how we relate to ourselves and others.

Most of us don't remember specific lessons; we remember the atmosphere. Did your father flinch at your hugs, or your mother praise your obedience but silence your emotion.

If we never stop to examine those formative moments, we end up playing them out again and again. We chase the same kind of love, react to the same kind of threat, or shut down before someone else can do it for us. Looking back isn't about blame. It's about breaking the pattern.

Understanding the influence of childhood helps us reframe our adult reactions as gay men. Instead of thinking, *What's wrong with me?* we can ask, *Where did I learn to do this?*

From a young age, I was different but not in any conspicuous way. I was neither too loud nor too quiet, neither too bold nor too shy. My difference was something that bubbled beneath the surface, something I couldn't quite put into words even if I had tried. It was in the way I formed friendships with girls who found my gentle, soft-spoken demeanour endearing. The girls were my sanctuary from the rougher games of the boys. The girls and I would chatter endlessly, play elaborate games and share secrets. Often the secrets were about the boys from whose behaviours the girls sought refuge.

However, I felt a strange pull towards those boys. I admired them. It wasn't the envious rivalry they showed towards each other. It was a yearning to be like them.

I was captivated by the older boys. I loved their confidence, their laughter, the way they moved with such careless freedom. More than anything, it was their physicality that drew my eyes to them time and again. I found myself fascinated by their legs: muscular and hairy. Mine were smooth and slender. I would watch their legs, pumping furiously as they raced down the football field or stretched out leisurely by the seaside as they rested, sun-soaked and carefree.

I felt a deep-seated longing to be close to them. I wanted to be part of their world of unspoken bonds and brotherly affections. I dreamt of having such strength, such visible markers of manhood. I imagined one day waking up to find my body transformed. I longed for my legs to sprout hair overnight and become robust and powerful. (This never happened, but I still love strong legs on a man.)

My admiration, however, was tinged with a confusing blend of feelings. I didn't just want to be like these boys. I felt drawn to them in a way I knew the boys were drawn to the girls. I caught myself staring too long. My cheeks flushed with heat and my heart beat faster whenever one of them accidentally brushed against me or threw a casual arm around my shoulder. I was thrilled and terrified by the sensation that I, in the naïveté of my young age, could not yet label as attraction.

A KINDNESS I WON'T FORGET

It wasn't until one fateful summer when an older cousin came to visit from Germany that my feelings began to crystallise into something more coherent. My cousin was everything I admired: tall and athletic, with legs covered in thick, dark hair. One afternoon, as we sat by the sea throwing pebbles into the water, he turned to me and asked, 'Do you have a girlfriend yet, Vinko?'

The question caught me off guard. My instinct was to deny or to deflect with a joke, but something in my cousin's earnest gaze made me pause.

'No,' I admitted, 'I don't think I want one.'

'Why is that?' my cousin prodded gently.

I hesitated and then, with the weight of my secret pressing down on me, I whispered, 'I think I like boys.'

My cousin's face remained unchanged, his smile kind and accepting. 'That's okay, Vinko. It's okay to feel that way. You're not alone in this.'

That conversation by the sea was the first time I had said it out loud. It didn't solve everything, but it cracked something open. My cousin's words gave me the courage to begin to embrace my identity. They helped me see that what I felt for those older boys wasn't just envy; it was attraction. That mattered. It made sense of what had confused me for so long. His kindness showed me that acceptance was possible, and that shaped how I saw myself.

Joining in

Early attractions are both powerful and confusing. I didn't know what to do with the feelings, so I buried them, tried to pass as someone I wasn't, and hoped it would all sort itself out. It didn't. I spent years watching from the sidelines, unsure how to take part, and wanting things I didn't understand. As I grew older, I began to navigate my complex feelings with a newfound confidence. When I started engaging with the gay community, I met men who had been through it, who didn't expect polish or performance.

Eventually, I stopped trying to be someone I wasn't. Those legs I used to fixate on weren't about masculinity; they were about belonging. I didn't become confident overnight, but I stopped pretending. I stopped shaping myself around other people's comfort and started figuring out what made sense to me. I was finally moving in my own direction.

For many gay men, early experiences of relationships can be tumultuous. In our business, we hear stories of early love, betrayal and trauma. Rage, fear and shame. Also, beauty. Why are gay men so affected by these early infatuations and experiences?

It's because we open up and explore feelings we had no idea existed or were so powerful. Although, I remember feeling attracted to men from a very early age. We are confused. Who are we and what kind of life might we expect to have? Life is unpredictable, impulsive and lacks clear direction.

I started exploring my sexuality much later in life than most gay men. I knew this was an important phase of my life. When

I decided I was ready, I knew exactly what direction to take. I remember my first experience of feeling romantic love blended with an erotic surge, how it consumed me and how I justified it to myself. Catholic guilt came along with it. In that first experience, there was the joy of touching a secret and feeling complete. It satisfied my inner self and my life. The darker side of these first experiences was the overwhelming shame that clouded and penetrated this powerful love.

Such early relationships shaped me. They taught me how quickly love could flip into shame, and how hard it was to separate the two. I learned to keep secrets, to read signals carefully, and to expect that something good might come with a cost. As I write this, I think of those early years, the lost too-short love stories that ended in tears and grief. They hurt and left their mark. Even the relationships that ended badly gave me a sense of possibility, however fleeting. In those early experiments, I connected in such powerful ways. An exciting journey.

TURNED DOWN AND TUNED IN

First love leaves a lasting imprint. I have had four significant relationships. Each one is a standout, one in a negative way, but a standout, nonetheless. My first significant gay relationship was with Oliver, a celebrity in London. I had no idea what was coming.

I arrived in London, still confused about my sexuality and deeply in love with a woman – she looked just like Julia Roberts, so let's call her JR. She was a strong, powerful, beautiful woman with whom I shared much in common and could easily see spending my life with. Ever the romantic, I had spent £10,000 on an engagement ring, the last of my money. Almost as soon as I arrived, I proposed to JR. She had the wisdom to turn me down. I was both heartbroken and relieved. I knew I was denying my sexuality by choosing the path of marriage. With her rejection, I was at the beginning of a new life. (I gave the ring to my mother.)

I found myself in London with little money and nowhere to live. Yet, wandering the cold, snowy streets, I felt free. I met a young man who introduced me to the world of theatre. This was life changing. I began working in the West End of London at the renowned Wyndham Theatre. The powerful performances and the vibrant world of live theatre enchanted me. Dame Diana Rigg, best known for her TV role as Emma Peel in *The Avengers*, was in the first play I helped with. She was starring as Medea in the Greek tragedy by Euripides. It was a fabulous time.

Although Oliver had a life partner and I was one of many young lovers, the experience transformed me. I learned about culture, society and the complexities of love and relationships. I was devastated when it ended, but its demise also prompted a period of immense growth. I realised that I had to embrace my identity and be openly gay. I found coming out difficult. It began with accepting myself, despite the societal pressures. And then I learned to show the world who I really was.

First love can leave you unprepared. It exposes what you want and what you're afraid of. People pretend it doesn't count because you're young. But it does. You carry that imprint into everything that follows. Whether you're trying to chase that feeling again or make sure you never feel that exposed, it shapes you. Whether you like it or not.

I grew up in a time when homophobia was embedded in the laws of many countries. England and Wales decriminalised homosexual acts in 1967, but social stigma was rife. In Australia, the laws were not changed until 1994, some 27 years later.

The struggles and traumas of those years didn't disappear. They became part of how I think, react and relate. I still notice their influence in what I avoid, how I trust and how I protect myself. The lessons weren't graceful, but they were valuable.

Not everyone experiences first love as being painful. Some people are lucky enough to be seen and held from the start. Others don't fall in love until much later. But first love always leaves an imprint, not because it is perfect but because it is pure. It shows us what our hearts are capable of before the world tells us to be careful.

I have spent much of my life pushing back against the pressure to be someone I'm not. Role models helped. They were friends, colleagues and older men in the community, people who had faced the same fears, made their way through it and didn't pretend otherwise. They asked the same questions and didn't flinch from the answers. Those role models have helped me change the way I understand myself. We don't choose how we start, but we can choose who we stand with and how we show up. For me, that took time and brought me to a version of life that feels real and earned.

My journey of self-discovery continues, even in my fifties, adding another layer to my understanding of who I am.

EVEN REPRESSED CHILDHOODS HAVE THEIR UPSIDES

Despite the social repression of homosexuality, growing up in the small seaside town of Kuna in Croatia during the 1970s was an experience steeped in love and kindness, an experience that I am profoundly grateful for every single day. Much of what I lived through in my youth has helped me in my journey of self-acceptance as a gay man. Afternoons helping my godmother or listening to the women gossip at the bakery while I waited for bread, seeped into my sense of what mattered. Not the dramatic moments, but the way people look after one another in small, unsentimental ways

Looking back, I see how my memories of Kuna shimmer with a kind of golden haze. Perhaps this is because these memories offer shelter from the confusion I carried inside. It was not a place where I could name who I was. But it was a place where I learned to notice beauty. The sea's gentle waves off the coast of Crkvice sang lullabies of comfort, and the sun kissed the earth with warmth and affection. I delighted in the cobblestone streets and quaint houses. They were the foundations of a community that I saw as bound together by genuine care and mutual respect. Of course, we had our share of petty jealousies and conflicts, but my childhood was mostly joy and resilience.

The people around me, from my family to my friends, contributed to a nurturing environment that allowed me to flourish. I had moments when understanding my feelings was like trying to catch the wind: elusive and perplexing. Perhaps others knew who I was before I did, because these moments were punctuated by acts of kindness and acceptance that made the path clearer. My cousin's understanding and acceptance. The laughter I shared with my friends. The older boys who showed me where I was heading, even if it turned out to be different from what I expected.

Kuna's breathtaking landscapes, close-knit community and festive village gatherings were blessings that I miss to this day.

Kindness, beauty and freedom are treasures that I carry with me always. Despite the societal norms that didn't understand or accept me, the treasures I experienced during my childhood provided me with a foundation of strength and resilience. It's what Andrea and I try to share with everyone we meet, in our business and beyond. Self-acceptance, if you can find it, will reward you with a life of joy.

CHAPTER NINE

Relationships and marriage

The referendum for marriage equality was a powerful time for so many Australians. Andrea and I, along with our clients and friends, felt deeply affected by the debates and discussions. One message I received from a friend profoundly resonated with me:

> Marriage equality is the only way to give everyone a choice and stop us discriminating against one another. It is the right step towards equality in general. It's not so much the marriage itself that concerns me. What I think is important is that we are all treated equally, so we are all looked upon in the same way, no matter who we choose to love.

Another friend, who understood the significance of the issue to me personally and my work at BBI, took the opposite view:

> Once marriage becomes the norm for everybody, you and I will be treated as a lesser being because we are not married. It's true that everyone will become equal in the sense of all having the same choices, but they are, in a sense, forced choices. The fact that marriage is

the normative, socially approved form means you are propelled towards it by social norms and structures. The category 'married' gives a stamp of official approval, but it simultaneously gives the stamp of disapproval to those who are not married. When you get married, you sign away all sorts of rights that you are not even aware of at the time. Your legal and financial responsibility towards the other goes on for life. Or even in death.

In this final chapter, I delve into the diverse dynamics of relationships and the institution of marriage, exploring their significance, the societal norms that influence them, and the unique challenges faced by the LGBTQIA+ community.

In a world where marriage has historically been defined by heteronormative standards, the fight for marriage equality represents more than legal recognition. It is about our broader struggle for acceptance and the right to love freely. It is a symbol of societal progress towards inclusivity and equal treatment for all.

By engaging with the themes presented in this chapter, I hope that you will gain a deeper understanding of the importance of love, acceptance and equality in building a more inclusive society. You will see how the fight for marriage equality is not just about the legal right to marry, but also about challenging societal norms and advocating for the freedom to live and love authentically.

I am in support of equality and gay marriage; I fight for it every single day. I have dedicated the last 15 years to helping like-minded gay men find love. It is a profound and very special role to have in people's lives.

After a bitter and often damaging debate, Australia legalised same-sex marriage on 9 December 2017. It took leadership from both the Liberal and Labor parties to succeed. I know Malcolm Turnbull, who was then the Prime Minister, because I worked as an assistant for his wife, Lucy Turnbull. I believe he felt that changes to marriage laws had to be implemented through a plebiscite and a referendum, otherwise these rights could easily be taken away once he was no longer in power. He understood the bitter debate that was coming but believed in the Australian public. He believed it would be a 'Yes' and I celebrate him every day for the courage it took, and for what he did for our community.

MORE VISIBLE, MORE TOLERANT

Australians are becoming more tolerant as gay men and women are more visible. After the plebiscite there was a surge in weddings, with nearly 6000 same-sex couples marrying within the first year of legalisation. This contributed to a huge economic boost, with an annual increase of $500–550 million in wedding-related spending, according a 2015 SBS news story, 'Gay marriage an economic boon for Australia'.

Demand grew for services such as venues, catering, photography and attire, prompting businesses to cater more inclusively to same-sex couples. The sight of same-sex couples marrying has become almost commonplace.

People are afraid of what they can't see. When people meet Andrea and me, they see that we love each other, and they love the fact that we do, no matter whether we are in Australia, Italy or Croatia. Love always wins, and everybody loves love.

Gay marriage makes us more visible, but we are still far from enjoying complete and equal acceptance. We have come a long way, but we still have a long way to go. And the risk of moving backward is ever present in today's fragile world; witness the rise of right-wing groups across the globe.

And there is still so much misrepresentation of gay relationships. How many movies show gay relationships in an open and affirming way? Not many. Yes, there are more gay relationships portrayed, but they often show troubled couples, or the gay couples play second fiddle to people in a heterosexual relationship. Despite the heartwarming nature of the relationship in the movie *Brokeback Mountain*, the sex is unconvincing.

We have a long way to go to develop equality in cultural images (in art, film, literature). For me, that's a much bigger problem than marriage laws. This is what we need to concentrate on: bringing equality to a visual platform to achieve acceptance.

Our clients talk about being despondent, depressed, and not recognised by their colleagues, their families and at times, by themselves. The social structures that construct heterosexuality as the norm are not just imposed from the outside. We internalise these norms, so society's judgement becomes our judgement against ourselves. This is a huge issue.

THE FRANTIC SEARCH FOR PLEASURE

The 'frantic search for pleasure' sits inside this frame of melancholic self-rejection. What I mean by this is the endless hook-ups and transitory relationships that are so entrenched in gay culture.

To be sure, pleasure without commitment is a rebellion against, or an antidote to, the depression or melancholy that many of us feel. And it is a form of defiance against the normative heterosexual idea of what life and love should be. It is a celebration of freedom from normative structures.

In the end, though, it does not satisfy or assuage the feeling that something is missing, from what some of our clients say to me. Many report that the intensity of the taboo pleasure and its excess is followed by the absence of acceptance, belonging, love, safety and affirmation.

There is, of course, a danger here. If the desire for a committed relationship stems from a desire to make up for self-rejection, which is largely unconscious, you will neither be able to love your partner and give him the affirmation he craves, nor accept his love as genuine. On this logic, finding a partner who wants commitment is only the beginning of a long struggle toward self-acceptance.

I believe there comes a time when we want to, in a way, settle down. This is a difficult concept to grasp in gay culture. I wonder what sense to make of this difficulty. Is it that the pursuit of orgiastic pleasure is intrinsic to avoiding self-doubt and judgement? Is it because we fear that the thrill of the chase just won't be there inside a steady relationship, and so our sexual desire will die?

As random sexual gratification gives way to learning how to love a man and accept his love in return, the trouble or danger becomes most stark. Love, of course, has many modes of expression, not just sexuality. But if a man's sexuality is in any way linked with self-rejection (which it most probably is), this transition may be fraught with difficulty. Add to that, the difficulty of learning to love in a culture that has almost no cultural representation of men loving men (as opposed to men having sex with men).

I hear men say so very often: 'At the end of the day, I come home alone', and that is what they don't want.

But what does it mean to have 'someone to come home to'. As I mentioned in Chapter 6, for some, it might mean someone to cook for them or with them, or someone to pour out their day's troubles to, or someone who keeps the home neat and tidy and for them.

I often wonder what image my clients have in their minds when they long for someone to come home to. Being on the other side – waiting for my partner to come home – isn't so lovely in my experience. In one of my relationships, I often experienced the daily goodbye as a daily sense of abandonment. And making something nice for someone 'to come home to' became a terrible form of loneliness, as I prepared the dinner and made the house beautiful and recovered from a hard day of work.

Being alone is fine if you don't have a problem with yourself. It is certainly better than the wrong relationship.

I have always believed that you must be happy alone before you can make a relationship work. That might be too simplistic, but it has worked for me. If I need my partner too much, I have a disaster on my hands; the chances are that my choice of partner is a mistake. It's not so much love that is blind but neediness that is blind, and unattractive to boot.

FIGHT THE NORMS TO GET WHAT YOU WANT

We evolve and learn who we are as we move through different relationships in our lives. In the end we know what we really want and what we don't want. I would not be able to do my job unless I had failed relationships and lessons learned along the way. Empathy and love are not enough to support my job; understanding what works for someone and what doesn't is just as important.

Be out, be comfortable with yourself, and be open with your friends and family. Be proud of your individuality and sexuality. Be proud of who you are.

So why do we hide? Is it melancholy self-rejection that lurks behind the glamorous exterior? Does this take us back to the burden we gay men carry for not fitting within the norms? If it is, then the only thing to do is change the norms. And that is a risky business. People are very attached to the norms. Their identity is embedded in them. Yet, confronting norms and finding ways to change them is what we must do to have the life and love we want.

First, recognise the norms. Then, examine the ways they lead you to undermine yourself. And finally, begin the long, complex process of changing them. Learning how to love oneself is a good place to start, but it would be naïve to think *They got married and lived happily ever after.*

NATURE OR NURTURE DOESN'T MATTER

Is sexual behaviour and being gay in our genes? Or is a great deal of our sexuality social. I read a laugh-out-loud study of mice that sheds some light on the debate. The researcher noticed that the mothers licked the anus of the male babies, but not the females. If the mother didn't lick the male babies, they didn't later engage in sexual 'mounting' behaviour. Conversely, if the researcher tickled the anus of the female babies with a paintbrush, they engaged in sexual mounting behaviour when they became sexually active. The biologist who did that research argued that you just can't separate the physical from the social; they are so intricately interdependent on each other. This is more complex than it seems.

I believe we are born to be anyone we want to be and to love anyone we want to love. To be free of constraints and choices is a wonderful way to live. It's a wonderful way to love. We focus too much on what is expected of us, who we are meant to be, what our role is, what our sexuality is, and who we should love. Too much energy is wasted on all this.

Some people suggest that gay boys miss out on the 'normal, healthy stages of adolescent development'. I sure feel that

I missed out on this in my growing-up years. However, in my professional and personal experience, these stages are a normative myth. Being a teenager is excruciating for everyone, not just gay boys, lesbian girls, or trans kids. Society tries to bend everyone to its expectations. The idea that girls and boys naturally love each other is a myth. It must be learned, and it is excruciating. Of course, there is all the trauma of being outside the normative categories. It is an incredibly complex puzzle, and it does my head in to try to make sense of it.

When it comes to being comfortable in a relationship, there is a paragraph in *The Velvet Rage* by Alan Downs[2] that really stands out for me when explaining how he feels as a gay man in a relationship:

> I know I am a man. I need to be loved. I also need to love myself. I need to feel strong and also to cry. I need to feel alive and to grieve my losses. I need to know that there is someone in this world who truly loves me. I need to love someone. I need a safe, stable, and committed home. Truth is, we need all these things much more than I need great sex. So why then do we as gay men in general mostly chase that sex thing? Can you explain this or share your thoughts on this as an outsider? What are your views? Am I right?

I agree with this beautiful description. All I would add is that just about everyone also wants to have great sex.

---

2 Alan Downs. *The Velvet Rage*, Lifelong Books, USA, 2004.

For me, the answer is that yoga and meditation help in the struggle toward self-affirmation and the affirmation of your loved one. As in the words of yoga teacher and bestselling author of *Yoga Girl*, Rachel Brathen:[3]

> Yoga and meditation teach you and give you goals to create space where you were once stuck. To unwind the layers of protection you've built around your heart. To appreciate your body and become aware of the mind and the noise it creates. To make peace with who you are. The goal is to love, well ... YOU.

I celebrate being outside the norm. Being outside the norm is hard but important work. The creative evolution of the world involves change. Without change, we have death. Our capacity to stand outside the norm breathes life into the world. Not that the whole burden of creative evolution should lie with gay men. But it can help to see the creative potential that lies in not conforming to the norms.

MARRIAGE IN MY LIFE

Andrea and I have registered our relationship, embracing the legal recognition it provides. We call each other husbands, not because of the legalities, but because it signifies our deep connection to each other and to the world. For us, it's a term

---

3 Rachel Brathen, *Yoga Girl*, Simon & Schuster, USA, 2014.

of endearment that captures the essence of our bond. It's cute and meaningful, like a special word or nickname for a loved one. Whether it's 'partner', 'spouse', 'soulmate', or 'husband', these terms reflect the unique and personal nature of each relationship.

Our relationship transcends the label of 'marriage'. What truly matters is the profound commitment we have to each other, a commitment that goes beyond any legal or societal framework. Our life together is built on a foundation of love, trust and mutual respect. We have faced challenges and celebrated triumphs, always standing by each other's side. No matter what the future holds, our dedication to one another remains unwavering.

CONCLUSION

Recognise the power of love and commitment in your relationships, regardless of the label society might impose. Embrace your unique bond and find the terms that best express your connection, whether that is marriage or not.

Strive for authenticity in your relationships. Challenge social norms that limit your understanding of love and commitment. Be open to learning and growing with your partner, supporting each other through life's challenges and joys.

Let's work towards a more inclusive and accepting world. Let's advocate for equality and visibility, not just for gay men but for everyone who struggles to find acceptance. Yes, celebrate the progress we have made, but remain vigilant and active in the ongoing fight for full equality and representation.

We must stop hiding our true selves behind society's expectations and start embracing our individuality. Stop settling for relationships that do not fulfill us and start seeking connections that resonate with our true selves. By doing so, we contribute to a more compassionate and understanding world, where love is celebrated in all its diverse forms.

The all-in ending

You, my dear friend, are standing at the threshold of a new beginning. As you close this book, take a moment to reflect on the journey you've just taken. You've learned that the key to a richer, more fulfilling relationship lies in being 'all in', and in the simple yet profound acts of listening to yourself and to your man.

Could it be that simple? Yes, it is. But it is not easy, as you now know from reading the long and winding journey that Andrea and I have been on.

Love between men is complicated by social stigma, health risks, the ups and downs of gay culture and, importantly, by the fast-flowing world of modern technology, with its disposable swipe-left-or-right dating apps.

In my experience, desire is at the heart of our need for real connection. Connection is the most potent aphrodisiac, the spiciest sex toy, and the wildest ride of your life. If you finish this book knowing this, my work is done. Your world will become full of endless possibilities. You will create meaningful connections and live a life full of love and adventure. You will navigate life's challenges with grace and achieve your goals with clarity and purpose.

But how can you reboot connection in your life? How can you find the path away from disposable relationships to an all-in approach?

I've said it all the way through this book, it is through the skill of listening. It is all too easy to underestimate this powerful ability, taught to me first by my grandmother as she held my hand in the woods around the small town of Kuna in Croatia, where I grew up. That's why I dedicated an entire chapter to the art and skill of listening.

Imagine if you will, my friend, waking up each day feeling connected, understood and at peace with who you are. Imagine all your relationships deepening, the conversations becoming more meaningful, and your outlook on life shifting from one of scarcity to one of abundance. Picture yourself surrounded by people who see you and appreciate you for who you are. They support your dreams. This is the life that awaits you when you take the principles from this book to heart.

Listen with your ears and with your heart. See possibilities in every situation. Approach every interaction with love and understanding. These are the foundations of true connection and fulfillment.

Listening, loving and understanding will help you navigate all of life's complexities:

- The friendships and family dynamics
- Your self-hatred and self-acceptance
- The social stigma, and health challenges.

Ultimately, you will arrive at jouissance, that exquisite French word that conveys pleasure beyond safety. The joys and sorrows of living life to the full.

I have shared all my secrets to love and happiness with you. I have held back nothing. You can follow the guidance of this book on your journey to find the love of your life. That said, if you want more assistance, Andrea and I are here to help you. We will listen to all that you hope for and want and guide you through the dating process, as we have done for so many men before you. We will believe in you as you learn to believe in yourself. We will laugh and cry and debrief with you, and help you fall in love with yourself again.

My wish is simple. For everyone who reads this book, I hope you will be able to create a life filled with love, understanding and endless possibilities. Because I know your love will ripple out, touching the lives of others and making the world a kinder, more connected place.

BEAU BRUMMELL INTRODUCTIONS

Beau Brummell Introductions (BBI) is a highly selective and personalised matchmaking agency for gay men. We have the largest private database of influential and inspiring single gay men in Australia, the United Kingdom, the United States (New York, Los Angeles, Miami, San Francisco and Chicago), Hong Kong, Singapore and New Zealand. We set out to help our clients meet their perfect match.

Andrea and I have helped over 1500 love stories blossom, which makes us so proud. For us, the measure of our success is when our couples stay together for 12 months, which is a high bar. Over 1400 couples have leaped that bar. And countless of our clients, still on the path to a lasting relationship, have learned to love *themselves* for the first time. And that is the most precious love any of us can find because, without it, we cannot truly let anyone else into our hearts.

As you will discover, the key to our success is our personal touch. We meet every one of our clients personally and get to know them. We discover more about their interests, tastes and values. We get to the heart of what each man is looking for out of life and in a partner, and then use our comprehensive database of clients to select suitable matches and arrange introductions.

And we coach our clients on how to overcome their history of disappointments and approach each new date with fresh eyes and an open heart.

The name Beau Brummell Introductions came about in the most unexpected way. After countless notes and brainstorming sessions, nothing ever quite felt right. Then one day, during a conversation with our friend Kelly Barber, who runs a marketing agency, she casually mentioned the name. In that instant, it clicked. It was the very first suggestion that sounded perfect – timeless, elegant, and capturing exactly what we wanted to represent.

Beau Brummell himself was an iconic 18th century figure, often remembered as the original arbiter of men's style. Known as a 'dandy', he wasn't just about fashion but about refinement, elegance, and setting the standard for how gentlemen carried themselves. Even today, so many things connected to men's style and sophistication can be traced back to him.

Looking back, I smile because Kelly probably doesn't even realise what a gift that moment was. After all the scribbled notes and late nights of searching for the right name, hers was the one that landed – and it has proven to be exactly right. It still feels like us. It carries the heart of what we do: bringing people together with care, intention, and a touch of timeless style.

ACKNOWLEDGMENTS

How does one begin?

It's always daunting to put into words the gratitude I feel, knowing I'll never be able to name everyone who deserves to be here. I am blessed beyond measure to have had so many wonderful souls shape my journey – friends, muses, teachers, lovers and family – each leaving an indelible mark on who I am today. My life has been a beautiful tapestry of chosen paths and chosen people, and I am deeply grateful to every single one of you who has walked beside me.

In my late thirties, life gifted me Andrea. Choosing to open my heart fully and give everything I had to our relationship remains the best decision I have ever made. Andrea, you have helped me discover my true self. You challenge me – often, passionately, as only an Italian can – and yet every conversation, every laugh, every disagreement leaves me stronger, softer, and more whole. To dance through life with you is my greatest joy.

To my immediate family – though not present in my life now, you will always live within me. My beautiful mama,

ACKNOWLEDGMENTS

Tanja, taught me generosity, kindness and the value of hard work. Her warmth and resilience shaped the person I am, and I carry the comfort of her love in my heart. My grandmother's lessons and my childhood on the land in Croatia rooted me deeply in family, heritage and belonging. My connection to that land and its people remains one of my greatest treasures.

To my Italian family – Mamma Zaza and the whole wonderful clan – thank you for embracing me so completely. Your love, laughter and chaos have made me feel at home in a new world. I am happiest when I am with you.

To my friends, my chosen family – you are my true anchors. The strong, inspiring women who have shared their wisdom, strength and love with me: Nadine Garner, Anita Smith, Ivana Goravica, Narelle Kellahan, Eileen Hall, Lili Hibberd, Baci Moore, Deborah Gray, Jodie Livingstone, Danijela Iacano, Karmen Dikovic, Lee Matthews, Therese Hunt, Jacquie Backer, Julie Reed, Kerry Ord, Karen Doughman, Benedetta Mazzini, Lucy and Daisy Turnbull, Mandy and Hayley McElhinney, Antonia Perricone Mrljak, Emma Cosgrove, Kelli Lee Andrews, Dubravka and Anita Kapor, Julija Zimonjic, Katie Collins, Ainslie Curren, Mia Hunter, Meg Gold, Kelly Barber, Sally Macpherson, Dunja Alexander, Rebecca Goldsworthy, Tannyson Logar, Andelka Budic, Zeljana Bilusica – whether our time together was brief or long, your presence has left a lasting imprint on my heart. Thank you for your guidance, laughter and unwavering belief in me.

And to all the men who have crossed my path – friends, partners and teachers alike – thank you for helping me grow, for grounding me, and for reminding me what it means to love and be loved. David Mathlin, Peter Curcuruto, Antoni Ostoja, Peter Mason, Cameron Barnett, Watthanapon Thomee, Keith Honhold, Raffaele Borriello, Joe Drew, Paulo and Vito Costa, Miro Leko, John Logan, Paul Webber, Andrew McFarlane, Allen Saltoon, Bernard Nadel, Ratko Goravica, Todd Cummins, Beppe Zaza, Marin Mimica, Sylveste Krief – each of you played a part in shaping my story. I am grateful for every chapter we shared.

A very special thank you to Bronwyn Davies, who began this book journey with me back in 2012. You gave me courage when I doubted myself and reminded me that we all have a story worth telling – and that mine was meant to be shared.

To my book coach, Kath Walters – thank you for challenging me in ways that terrified me at times but ultimately made me better. Without your sharp guidance, these stories might have remained scattered memories rather than a book.

To Bernadette Foley – thank you for believing in *All In* exactly as it was meant to be. You were the only person in the publishing world who didn't try to reshape it into something else, and that trust gave me peace and confidence from the very first moment we met.

To Mel Feddersen, for creating the beautiful cover and design – how does one ever choose to put their own face on a book cover? We got there in the end.

Thanks to my two right hands at Beau Brummell Introductions, Katrina Williams and Valeria Diverio, whose unwavering support, creativity and patience carry me every day.

ACKNOWLEDGMENTS

To my publicist, Nicole Webb – thank you for believing that my story has a voice worth sharing. Your passion and faith in this journey mean the world to me.

Sealy Brandt – the best photographer one could ever have – for this cover shot and continuous support at Beau Brummell Introductions.

To all the 'critics' who read the early drafts and the first edit of *All In* – thank you. Your honesty, your courage to challenge, and your commitment to truth sharpened every page. You reminded me that growth is born from friction, and that love – in writing and in life – demands we stay open even when it's uncomfortable. Your voices helped me see more clearly, write more deeply, and stand more firmly in what this book is meant to say. *All In* is stronger because of you.

And finally, to the gay community and to every client who has trusted me through Beau Brummell Introductions – thank you. You have given me the privilege of doing what I love most: creating love and connection. You've allowed me to live my truth, to build a career rooted in empathy and authenticity, and to witness the beauty of love in all its forms. Being a gay man is the greatest gift – thank you, God, for creating us with such brilliance and heart.

With love and gratitude,

Vinko

Ohh, and who could forget Monte? Thank you for all the furry cuddles and puppy love, and Marco Mengoni for all the music while writing away …

www.ingramcontent.com/pod-product-compliance
Lightning Source LLC
Chambersburg PA
CBHW061207070526
44583CB00025B/3146